Radin draws on her extensive scholarship and experience to produce a book that will be very valuable for those entering, or considering entering, the increasingly diverse field of policy analysis. By conveying the many contexts in which policy analysts practice, the book's cases will help aspiring analysts better match their personal values to the varieties of roles available in the policy making process.

David L. Weimer, University of Wisconsin–Madison, USA

Radin's engaging approach presents policy analysis as highly diverse, in terms of what advisors/analysts do from positions in and outside government, and in terms of the clients they serve. With insightful cases, the book does great justice to major challenges to policy analysis in the everyday practice of policy advice across the globe.

Marleen Brans, KU Leuven Public Governance Institute,
Belgium and Vice-President of the International Public Policy Association

The field of Public Policy Analysis has increasingly drawn upon abstract models of technical analysis oblivious to practical relevance to public problem-solving and to the challenges involved in wading through the increasingly complex policy world. Beryl Radin, with the distillation of the rich experience of her career as a "pracademic," combined with a set of masterfully crafted cases, presents an insightful and highly readable account of how Public Policy Analysis can best be studied and practiced in response to challenges of the twenty-first century world.

Wai-Fung Lam, University of Hong Kong, China

As a public policy consultant for multinational organizations, I have been involved in programs that provide policy recommendations to governments at all levels of China. If I had seen a book like Prof. Beryl Radin's during my academic career, I would have been more prepared to deal with the issues that occurred at work.

Lina Li, Central University of Finance and Economics, China

Policy Analysis in the Twenty-First Century

The field called policy analysis focused originally on the formulation of new policies and was structured to give advice to those in the top reaches of government agencies. Within several decades the field moved beyond the formulation stage of the policy process (creating new policies) to agenda setting, implementation and evaluation of existing policies. New skill sets emerged and staff were found in many parts of the policy world. Despite these changes, there has been little attention paid to the possible shifts in the relationship between analysts and clients, and students of policy analysis often enter the world of work with little exposure to the situations they might face. *Policy Analysis in the Twenty-First Century* is designed to familiarize students with the diversity of experiences that they can expect to face in their practitioner role.

Author Beryl Radin bases the discussion on case studies that illustrate realities in the current policy analysis environment. Set in very different environments (including both US and international settings), the players in the cases illustrate three different stages of a career (beginning the career, mid-career, and people at the end of their career). The cases are based on realistic situations and demonstrate the volatility and complexity of the decision environments. At the same time, they provide attention to the analysts' personal values and career goals. This book will be required reading for faculty and masters level students in both public management and policy analysis classes. It may also be used in executive programs.

Beryl A. Radin is a member of the faculty of the McCourt School of Public Policy at Georgetown University, USA. An elected member of the National Academy of Public Administration, she was the Managing Editor of the *Journal of Public Administration Research and Theory* and also served as the editor of a book series on Public Management and Change at Georgetown University Press. Her government service included two years as a Special Advisor to the Assistant Secretary for Management and Budget of the US Department of Health and Human Services. Professor Radin has written a number of books and articles on public policy and public management issues. She received the 2014 International Research Society for Public Management Routledge Prize for Outstanding Contribution to Public Management Research, the John Gaus Award from the American Political Science Association in 2012, the H. George Frederickson Award for Lifetime Achievement from the Public Management Research Association in 2009, and the 2002 Donald Stone Award given by the American Society for Public Administration's section on intergovernmental management to recognize a scholar's distinguished record. Radin has been a past president of the Association of Public Policy Analysis and Management.

Policy Analysis in the Twenty-First Century

Complexity, Conflict, and Cases

Beryl A. Radin

Routledge
Taylor & Francis Group

NEW YORK AND LONDON

First published 2019
by Routledge
52 Vanderbilt Avenue, New York, NY 10017

and by Routledge
2 Park Square, Milton Park, Abingdon, Oxon, OX14 4RN

Routledge is an imprint of the Taylor & Francis Group, an informa business

© 2019 Taylor & Francis

The right of Beryl A. Radin to be identified as author of this work has been asserted by her in accordance with sections 77 and 78 of the Copyright, Designs and Patents Act 1988.

Library of Congress Cataloging-in-Publication Data
A catalog record for this title has been requested

ISBN: 978-0-367-22542-1 (hbk)
ISBN: 978-0-367-22543-8 (pbk)
ISBN: 978-0-429-27810-5 (ebk)

Typeset in Goudy
by Wearset Ltd, Boldon, Tyne and Wear

Contents

Acknowledgments

The ever-changing field of public policy means that faculty members inevitably learn from their students. Students bring their current and past experience into the classroom and provide faculty with new ideas. This is particularly true when students have one foot in the classroom and the other in the world of practice. This book developed from conversations with both pre-service and midcareer students over nearly a half century. In addition, my personal excursions into the practitioner world have given me a sense of that world. As a result, I am indebted to many people for both my suggestions in this volume and the cases that illustrate my advice.

Introduction

I enrolled in a PhD program at the University of California at Berkeley just about the time that the public policy program was created there. Berkeley (now the Goldman School) was one of the early academic institutions that developed an MPP (Masters of Public Policy) degree to follow the creation of a practitioner field in the US federal government in the 1960s. While my degree wasn't formally in public policy, like the field itself I too had my initial introduction to it wearing a practitioner's hat. But that Bay Area perch – overlooking the San Francisco Bay – was a productive place to watch the development of the field and to work with people who conceptualized the practice and teaching of policy analysis.

During the nearly 50 years that have elapsed I have watched the field of policy analysis develop from several vantage points. While most of those years were spent in an academic setting, I continued my practitioner orientation both inside and outside the university. I have taught in many different universities both in the US and abroad and have always been attracted to working with students who bring their practitioner orientation to the classroom. That has occurred in a number of US institutions as well as programs in other countries. These included Australia, India, Denmark, Israel and Hong Kong. I've also spent time inside the world of practice, sometimes as a consultant and other times as a staff member.

Over the years I have watched the field change. Many different demands have been made on it; the academic field has grown from a few institutions providing MPP degrees to a significant increase in both programs and graduates. Some changes have made their way into the journals and course syllabi but others have stayed in the world of practice. Over the years I have tried to bring both of those worlds into my classroom. I've tried to provide students with an understanding of both theory and practice, hoping that will help them become effective and useful advisors to decisionmakers, wherever and whoever they may be. As I have written this book, I have envisioned past conversations with students. I hope that their concerns are reflected in these pages.

But as Francis Fukuyama has written recently, "Public policy education is ripe for an overhaul" (Fukuyama, 2018). In an essay in *The American Interest*, he comments: "Being skilled in policy analysis is woefully inadequate to bring about policy change in the real world." He notes that the current educational experience in policy analysis focuses on the development of an optimal policy, not on how to achieve that outcome. Fukuyama highlights the need for three skills: Problem definition, solutions development and implementation.

My experience brings me to a perspective that is similar to Fukuyama's. But I add another development to my analysis. I point to the dramatic changes that have occurred in the world that have challenged the original view of the policy analysis field. The basic relationship between a decisionmaker (the client) and an analyst has moved from a two-person encounter to an extremely complex and diverse set of interactions. Clients are not only individuals but also networks and other collectivities of decisionmakers who cross organizational lines. Analysts are not only individuals who can apply quantitative methods to issues but people who seek to create approaches that seem to respond to the complexity they face. Environments are not simply expressed in traditional bureaucratic hierarchical structures but in relationships that transcend national boundaries and almost always involve political pressures. Issues can be defined with some clarity but are also expressed in competing ways that make it difficult to frame the policy problem. Information can be found in neat data systems but also discovered in a wide range of both formal and informal sources. And values and criteria can be identified but frequently represent conflicting views and perspectives that make a preferred state more difficult to define.

Thus while the basic relationship between a decisionmaker and an analyst does continue to fit some of the traditional realities of the policy analysis field, there are significant changes that are now found in the practice of policy analysis within the twenty-first century that limit the effectiveness of these traditional approaches. These changes represent a challenge to the field and call for new ways for analysts to provide advice to decisionmakers.

Despite these changes, there has been little self-consciousness in the field about the possible shifts that may have occurred in the relationship between analysts and clients. Few faculty even raise the issues. Students have tended to focus on the technical analytical techniques employed and the curriculum emphasizes those techniques. Fewer and fewer faculty members have practitioner experience that they bring to the classroom. Students enter the world of work with little exposure to the situations they might face. As a result, it has become more difficult for graduates of public policy programs to create a career path for themselves.

This is the setting which this volume attempts to address.

This volume seeks to help students answer the following question: How has the field responded to the diversity of clients, analysts, issues, information and goals in a way that limits confusion but has stimulated creativity and a willingness to define the field in new ways? My motivation in writing this book is not to focus on the general and abstract but to acknowledge the specific and variability. It is my view that this is the way to empower a new generation of policy analysts.

What Can We Learn from Cases and Examples?

This is not a book that seeks to challenge the continued relevance of works by writers such as Weimer and Vining (1992), Bardach and Patashnik (2016) or Hogwood and Gunn (1984). These works continue to be important. Rather, it focuses on a range of policy problems that don't seem to fit the assumptions of the past. Issues that are usually viewed as a part of the background of the analysis have moved to the foreground. As such, they demand a shift in the way we think about these topics.

Here are a few examples. We begin with the assumption that clients are likely to be multiple and conflicting. We assume that the political environment of an issue is both crucial but always changing. We are likely to operate without face-to-face encounters with the decisionmaker we are meant to advise. We do not search for comprehensive change but for incremental change. Our sources of information are not always based on quantitative data but may stem from hunches and observations as well. We assume that analysts bring their own values and experiences to the table; they search for a career structure but are willing to try new things. Their recommendations don't always appear in a written memo but can be found in new processes and interpersonal relationships within an organization and with their colleagues.

These examples may challenge the views of some people who are likely to define themselves as policy analysts. They are particularly problematic for those who find themselves operating in an era when political leaders find it difficult to define "facts." It is probably not an accident that the policy analysis field hasn't spent a lot of time developing a code of ethics for itself.

It will be clear to most readers that the cases that are included in this volume pose problems and demands that are far from "right answer" responses. Each of the cases that is used has a number of appropriate answers that flow from the personal expectations of the analyst and the client as well as the complexity of the institutional setting and players involved. (*The information from the cases is presented in each chapter in italics*).

The cases: It seemed to me that the best way to present this alternative view of policy analysis was through the use of a group of cases to illustrate the contemporary issues I have observed. I have written 20 cases that collectively support my perspective. The cases are fictionalized but based on real situations. Neither the analyst nor the decisionmakers are based on identifiable individuals. Some are composites of the experience of several people. Others are fictionalized versions of students and friends I have known over the years. As I have written the pages that follow, I have envisioned the characters in my cases as my students, my colleagues and my friends.

I have created fictional characters in several of my earlier books. In only one case did I encounter a person who came up to me and said, "I am John!" (a character in one of my books). I responded: "No, you are not John." But he was partially right!

The cases illustrate the following diverse patterns:

Location: More than half of the cases are set in the US but in different settings and involving different issues. More than a third of the cases are placed in non-US settings and are found in multinational organizations as well as different government locations across the globe.

The main actor: Most of the cases focus on the role of the policy analyst while a few focus on the decisionmaker/client. Half of the main actors are men and half are women. Approximately one-third of the main actors are in the early stages of their career, one-third in mid-level positions, and one-third approaching retirement.

Advocate vs. analyst: Approximately half of the actors have a personal commitment to the policy area. As a result, that seems to make them more of an advocate than someone who has a purely analytic perspective.

Attributes of the client: More than half of the actors are faced with a complex client or multiple clients. As such there is not a single pathway that would satisfy these diverse clients.

Attributes of the environment: Most of the cases are set in environments that are turbulent, conflictual and constantly changing. They require the type of policy analysis that deals with conflicting values and multiple goals.

Information used: Many of the cases involve information or analytic work that is viewed as helpful but not adequate to deal with the policy problem.

The Structure of the Book

The eight chapters in this volume are structured around three goals. The first section of each chapter describes the changes that have taken place over the years in the subject discussed. The second section characterizes the issues that have emerged in the early decades of the twenty-first century. And the third section provides examples of these issues that are drawn from the case studies.

Chapter 1, *The Development of the Policy Analysis Field*, traces the development of the policy analysis field from its formal origins in the US in the 1960s. It emphasizes the relationship between the advisor and the decisionmaker and examines how it has changed over the years as the policy analysis function has developed and modified. It highlights the globalization of the field, moving from a set of activities mostly limited to the US to a variegated activity with very different behaviors that by the twenty-first century represent international political cultures, structures and expectations.

Chapter 2, *Clients: A Moving Target*, begins with the practice of identifying clients because of their positions as individuals with formal authority who are located on the top rungs of a public organization. The definition of "client" began to change as participants in the policymaking world found that the formal hierarchical bureaucratic structure does not always describe the real decision-making process in a governmental agency. Shared authority has become more common and thus a single individual client may not have the sole authority to act on analytic advice. These actors may involve players across different levels of government who have a legitimate role in the policy process. These multiple players moved beyond governmental entities to involve nongovernmental agencies who are linked together in networks that may be both formal and informal in nature.

Chapter 3, *The Analyst: Expectations and Constraints.* Policy analysts emerge from many different institutions of higher education; they write for a number of journals and other publications, are the focus of national and international organizations, and continue to generate debate about the parameters of its research subjects and methodologies. Yet there is a lack of clarity about its dimensions and jobs with the label "policy analyst" being found in many settings.

There is not a single definition of the term "policy analyst" that would be agreed to by all of the players in either the academic or practitioner settings. Many of them (such as Vining and Weimer) would differentiate between analysis and research and there is a complicated relationship between the analyst's personal values and expectations and those embedded in the position itself.

Chapter 4, *The Policy Environment: Increasing Acknowledgment of Complexity.* In the early days of the field it was rare to find explicit attention to the impact of the structure and the political process within the US. While that structure and process produced policies that when adopted often required substantive trade-offs at the implementation stage, there was a tendency to avoid thinking seriously about implementation requirements during adoption. New programs rarely emerged from the policy adoption stage of the policy process with the clarity that was more likely to emerge from a parliamentary system. Pressman and Wildavsky's (1973) graphic depiction of the complexity of joint action has become even more complex over the years. The trade-offs that did emerge often produced conflicting values and approaches within the policy design that emerged from the extended political policy adoption process.

Fewer agencies (particularly those in the US) had environments that operated through predictable hierarchical relationships. New organizational forms emerged. Policy environments ranged from stable relationships to highly turbulent settings in which advocates of different approaches could be expected to emerge in policy discussions. Analysts are challenged to find ways to map the actors and issues involved as well as their relationships.

Chapter 5, *The Policy Issue Itself,* focuses on those attributes that seem to be embedded in the activities associated with a particular policy sector. We are more likely to discover it when we focus on those who actually provide the service. Many policy fields seem to deal with those attributes when they define the professional discretion that is present in a sector. Specialization in a distinct policy area is a way to indirectly focus on those unique attributes.

These differences are often embedded in the attributes of the sector and analysts can find them by paying attention to those attributes. It is likely that a one-size-fits-all approach will not help an analyst comprehend the predictable dynamics found in the issue. This is especially true in a democratic society which is likely to produce very few policy issues in which there is agreement on the next steps to take to deal with a national policy problem.

Chapter 6, *Information and Evidence*, is a topic that has become much more complex in the decades that have elapsed since the practice of policy analysis began. We have given attention to the definition of information, the kinds of information that are appropriate, sources of information, the need for it, as well as its functions and uses. In many ways we have become much more sophisticated about the limits of the original views that were embedded in the conceptual paradigms and analytic approaches used by the early analysts.

At the same time, policy analysts have increasingly defined their role around the use of complex quantitative analytic techniques. Such a condition may push the analyst away from the specific needs of a client or the unique demands of the policy problem at the core of the assignment. Use of these techniques can collide with the principles that are linked to the values of the scientific method and a constant search for evidence that questions existing recommendations.

Chapter 7, *Criteria and Values*, reflects the strong commitment in the policy analysis field to provide alternative options that the client might consider to address the policy problem. Options are related to choice and emerge from the values of a democracy. They provide the analyst with some creative space to think about different approaches to the policy problem.

This is important because many policy issues that have emerged in the twenty-first century represent new developments within the society, are constantly changing, are a combination of policy problems or stem from the addition of new players or new issues in the policy environment. They call out for approaches that might seem to be "out of the box" and often contain elements that are viewed as contradictory.

Two approaches are included in this chapter. One involves items that rest on the presence of more than one value. It is not surprising that the classic categorization of *effectiveness, efficiency* and *equity* values emerges in issues that involve multiple and contradictory values.

The second approach revolves around the need to define criteria that are likely to be considered by the decisionmaker (or decisionmakers) in making a choice. The classic criteria include four different categories: *Cost, effectiveness, political feasibility* and *implementability*. The analyst not only needs to define these criteria but also find a way to weight them in terms of their importance to the client. Acknowledging the different perspectives that will emerge from multiple clients will set the scene for trade-offs between alternatives.

Chapter 8, *A Checklist*, provides the book's reader with an approach that can structure the range of topics that might respond to many of the challenges found in policy analysis in the twenty-first century. While there is no "right" answer to these items and issues, this list offers policy analysts an opportunity to anticipate possible problems that emerge from the cases included in this volume.

It is my hope that the seven items covered in the book will provide a point of departure for future policy analysts. It has been written as an attempt to address the gap found in much of the literature and provide a way to move to new strategies to confront the complex issues described in this discussion.

1 The Development of the Policy Analysis Field[1]

Introduction

Unlike most academic and research fields, the policy analysis field does not operate as an independent and separate endeavor. By definition, policy analysis involves a conversation between an analyst and a decisionmaker or a decision-making process. From its earliest days in the 1960s as a professional field of practice, that conversation has been the form in which advice has been transmitted from someone who is viewed as an expert on a specific topic to someone else who has been charged with making a decision about something related to that topic. The process that emerges from this task is one of advising that decisionmaker (usually called the client of the analyst). The analyst employs a wide range of information sources derived from multiple methodologies to help decisionmakers exert whatever power, authority or influence is available to them. At its broadest definition, thus, public policy analysis can be viewed as advice to decisionmakers somewhere involving the public sector. While that sector differs across the globe, the relationship between analysts and their clients involves many common processes and issues.

Despite this interdependency between analysts and clients, the field rarely talks about the role and importance of that conversation and has paid very little attention to what is a two-way process. It is a topic that almost never shows up in the policy journals or in panels at policy conferences. The focus of the field has been on the assumptions, tools, roles and reality of the analyst and little acknowledgment that the analyst is an *advisor* to the decisionmaker – not the decisionmaker himself or herself.

The current experience involving policy advising has moved the field from one that had been found largely in the US to include experience within other countries, some of which have focused on the advising function. It illustrates similarities and differences that emerge from diverse political, cultural and organizational settings. This range of policy settings indicate both positive and negative experiences with the advising function. These cases of past experience illustrate the potential as well as the problems attached to the advising relationships. This chapter reviews the role of the client in three policy analysis eras and places that role within the broader history of the policy analysis field.

Difficulty Defining the "Client"

While a broad definition of the relationship between the analyst and a decisionmaker or client does provide a context for the policy analysis function, it is used in many different ways. It is not always clear what it means to be either a "decisionmaker" or a "client" of policy analysis. Is the decisionmaker someone who has authority or influence on a particular policy question? Is the client someone who pays directly or indirectly for the analytic work that is done? Or is the client someone who is affected by the policy decision? Are we talking about an individual decisionmaker or are we also focusing on multiple players who operate within a network or are involved in various decision-making processes? All of these possibilities (and others) are likely to arise when one tries to define the recipient of policy advice (Radin, 2013).

But the field of policy analysis has tended to minimize attention to the role and changes related to the recipient of advice. The concept of a "client" – if it is used at all – is rarely discussed in much detail. Weimer and Vining do define policy analysis as advice to a client (Weimer and Vining, 1992); Geva-May with Wildavsky (Geva-May and Wildavsky, 1997) emphasized the role of the client, and others deal with the client as a stakeholder. The policy analyst function has changed quite dramatically over the years because of modifications in the context of the effort as well as changes in the training and experience of working policy analysts. As a result there is little attention to the role of the decisionmaker-client and its changes and expectations as the field has been modified. While the decisionmaker-client often seems to be present in the depiction of the policy analysis process, that role is presented in the form of shadowy figures who are defined – if at all – by players within a bureaucratic organizational structure. It is time to look at the relationship between the advisor and the decisionmaker and examine how it has changed over the years as the policy analysis function has developed and modified. It is particularly important to investigate this issue as the policy analysis field has developed globally, moving from a set of activities mostly limited to the US to a variegated activity with very different behaviors that by the twenty-first century represent international political cultures, structures and expectations. The formal policy analysis field has tended to avoid depicting the role of analysts as advisors even though the top civil servants in most parliamentary systems are usually defined as individuals who give advice to high-level decisionmakers. The top civil servant in the British TV series "Yes Minister" is depicted as the elite actor advisor who often finds ways of manipulating the political decisionmaker. While the classic parliamentary approach has not emphasized formal analysis tied to research as the basis for the advice, few have picked up the differences between the US shared power system and the Westminster system in this regard.

Although the first book on policy analysis in the US included a chapter entitled "Clients" (Meltsner, 1976) subsequent volumes such as the multiple editions of Bardach's *A Practical Guide for Policy Analysis* (the most recent volume has a co-author: Bardach and Patashnik, 2016) do not focus on the client role. It is as if the client stays in the shadows. Instead, attention has been concentrated on the methodologies and theories employed by the analyst, rarely focusing attention on the changes and expectations of those who are being advised. In large part this has occurred as the field of policy analysis has moved from a field of practice to an academic subject with both undergraduate and graduate programs charged with training future analysts. But it also relates to the constant change that has occurred over those 50 years in the types of client we are trying to advise and their expectations about the advising process.

As a result the normal tensions between the expectations of the analyst and the realities experienced by the decisionmaker have grown and there have been increased gulfs between the two players in the basic advising conversation. Indeed, it is often hard to differentiate between the two roles in the advising process. Analysts forget that they have not been provided with the authority to make decisions and believe that their technical expertise should be the sole basis for decisions. Decisionmakers often feel that analysts do not understand the constraints they experience and thus are present only to help them justify their already determined decisions. It seems that both sets of actors have lost their way in the process. The result of this situation is that the policy analysis profession has not achieved the expectations that were embedded in its formation and, instead, decisionmakers revert to the ideological and political processes of the past.

While there are examples of useful relationships between analysts and clients, it does not appear that these examples have informed either participant in the policy conversation. It is useful to illustrate the dimensions of the problems experienced by both groups by looking at the changing context in which this activity takes place and by analyzing the changes in the role of the client by presenting their expectations in three consecutive eras in the US.

This chapter reviews the expectations during the early stages of the policy field in the 1960s. It analyzes the shifts that occurred in the period between the 1970s and 1990s. It examines the changes that have occurred in the early years of the twenty-first century, particularly the impact of globalization and politicization. And despite the changes that have occurred over the past half century, behaviors and expectations from earlier eras continue today. Each of these eras illustrates different expectations about the analytical approaches to analysis, the organization of the policy analysis profession, modes of educating individuals in university settings, and whether clients expect their advisors to employ analytical or advocacy approaches to issues. While changes have occurred in these three eras, the field of policy analysis has not replaced any of the past approaches and thus examples of all three approaches are found today. As such, policy analysis in the twenty-first century continues to contain approaches that were developed in earlier periods.

The Role of the Policy Analyst in History

The field of policy analysis developed as both a field of practice and an academic field in the 1960s. But while it developed as a distinct profession and academic field at that time, the practice of providing policy advice to decisionmakers is really an ancient art. Some have noted that Machiavelli might have been the first policy analyst in his role as an advisor to the Prince but there were even earlier expressions of this role across the globe. Joseph in the Old Testament has been described as a first advisor to the Pharaoh. Few of us know these people but these are individuals who performed the timeless functions of friend, educator, conscience, eyes and ears, executor and advisor to often isolated and lonely rulers (Goldhamer, 1978, p. ix). Indeed, although western political thought has tended to emphasize the role that Machiavelli played as advisor to the Prince above all others, Goldhamer notes that others – namely, early Chinese, Indian and Greek writers – have also reflected on their experience as counselors to rulers and other decisionmakers" (Goldhamer, 1978, p. 8; Bondanella and Musa, 1979, p. 154).

There are other lessons from the past that help us understand the attributes of the policy analysis field that took shape in the early 1960s. Goldhamer emphasizes the use of history and experience as a major source of wisdom and describes the replacement of clergy by jurists/ lawyers (Goldhamer, 1978, p. 22). He notes the skepticism through the years about the ability of youthful – rather than elder – advisors to provide effective counsel, citing Aristotle's observation that "youths do extremely well in mathematics but that young men of practice wisdom are difficult to find" (Goldhamer, 1978, p. 23).

Though the ruler may be motivated to seek additional sources of information, Goldhamer suggests that one must limit the number of advisors who provide counsel. He quotes the advice of Kautilya, the tutor and first minister of Chandragupta, founder of the fourth-century BC Maurya dynasty in India: "The king should consult three or four ministers. Consultation with a single minister may not lead to any definite consultation in cases of complicated issues" (Goldhamer, 1978, pp. 94–5).

The Role of the Client in History

One can see the changes that have occurred in the role of the client by presenting them in three consecutive eras. Because policy analysis tended to be a field found almost exclusively in the US during both Eras 1 and 2, one sees that the self-consciousness in the field rarely paid attention to different approaches that were found in other political systems. Era 1 is the creation of the field in the 1960s. Much of the literature that we continue to use stays at this initial era. Era 2 is the expansion of the field to the 1990s. And Era 3 involves globalization and politics today.

The original concept of the client of the policy analyst was an individual who has authority and is usually located on the top rungs of a public organization. Meltsner's depiction of four types of policy analysts with both political and technical skills did acknowledge different roles played by clients as well as different expectations about the relationship between analyst and client (Meltsner, 1976). But even Meltsner's description seemed to assume that the policy analyst would have a quasi-monopoly role in that advising process. By the end of the twentieth century, the image of the policy analyst as the advisor to the Prince (as in Machiavelli) was replaced by an image of an individual operating (usually in a public organization) along with other policy analysts in both public and non-public organizations.

Each era has devised different approaches that emerge from different types of policy issues, the diverse relationships between analysts and clients, the types of analysis required, its time frame, the stage of the policy process where it occurs, where in the system it occurs (e.g., whether it takes place inside government or outside government), the impact of the structure of the government involved, the placement of analysis in central agencies vs. program agencies, whether analysts and clients are career or political actors, the appropriate skill set found in analysts, and the boundaries between policy analysis and management.

Era 1. Although advice giving and advice seeking were hardly new, American society had experienced a significant change in the period after World War II. During the Progressive Era and especially during the New Deal, lawyers played a very important role as advisors in the US system. The shifts that had taken place in the legal profession (especially at Harvard Law School) broadened the legal field, formalized it and provided a way for lawyers to think of ways to use data and scientific information in their work. And their status within governmental agencies made their advising role very important.

But in the post-World War II period, social scientists began to play a role in the decision-making process. The imperatives of war had stimulated new analytic techniques – among them systems analysis and operations research – that sought to apply principles of rationality to strategic decision-making. Although still in an embryonic form, the computer technology of that period did allow individuals to manipulate what were then considered large data sets in ways that had been unthinkable in the past.

Yehezkel Dror, one of the earliest advocates for the creation of policy analysis as a new profession, described the early phases of this search for new expressions as "an invasion of public decision-making by economics" (Dror, 1971, p. 117). Further, he wrote, "Going far beyond the domain of economic policymaking, the economic approach to decision-making views every decision as an allocation of resources between alternatives, that is, as an economic problem" (Dror, 1971, p. 117).

All of this took form in the components of the Planning, Programing, and Budgeting System (PPBS), a decision allocation process that was established in the Department of Defense in 1961 and eventually extended by President Lyndon Johnson to other parts of the federal government. The analytic approach would always be closely associated with the style and interests of President John Kennedy's Secretary of Defense, Robert McNamara.

PPBS itself had antecedents in the work of the RAND Corporation in Santa Monica, California, the non-profit organization created in 1948, just after World War II was over, to do analytic work for the government, especially the DoD (RAND home page). The link to the RAND experience was obvious when McNamara asked former RAND staffer Charles Hitch to establish a Systems Analysis Unit with responsibility for the PPBS process. Today, almost 40 years since its initial implementation, PPBS continues to have both advocates and detractors (West, 2011).

The PPBS system that was put into place had at least three different goals. First, it sought to create opportunities for control by top agency officials over fragmented and diffuse organizational and program units. Despite the organization chart, the DoD was clearly a federal department that operated more like a feudal system than a tight bureaucratic hierarchy. The separate services – Army, Navy and Air Force – were distinct and separate units with their own programs, cultures and constituencies. The PPBS system sought to look at the DoD as a unity and to provide advice to the secretary; it represented a way for the secretary to establish control over hitherto decentralized operations and to identify crosscutting programs and issues within the highly fragmented department.

Second, the PPBS system was an attempt to improve efficiency in the way that resources were allocated and implemented. When DoD was examined from a centralized vantage point and functional categories across the department were defined, it was obvious that there were overlaps and redundancies within the multiple units, particularly in the procurement process. For example, economic efficiencies were not served by processes that could not define areas of economies of scale.

Third, the PPBS process rested on a belief that increased use of knowledge and information would produce better decisions. The experience of World War II was a heady one; advances in the availability and pro-duction of information gave the PPBS proponents the sense that it was possible to differentiate the false from the true and that the conceptual models they relied on would produce accurate and appropriate informa-tion (Radin, 2000).

The office that was established in the DoD to carry out McNamara's analytical agenda became the model for future analytic activity through-out the federal government. As the office developed, its goal of providing systematic, rational and science-based counsel to decisionmakers included what has become the classic policy analysis litany: Problem identification, development of options or alternatives, delineation of objectives and criteria, evaluation of impacts of these options, estimate of future effects, and – of course – recommendations for action.

In many ways, the establishment of this office represented a top-level strategy to avoid what were viewed as the pitfalls of traditional bureau-cratic behavior. Rather than move through a complex chain of command, the analysts in this office – regardless of their rank – had direct access to the top officials in the department. Those individuals became the clients of the analysts. Their loyalty was to the secretary of the department, the individual at the top of the organization (the Ruler in Machiavelli's formulation) who sought control and efficiencies in running the huge department. In addition to the PPBS system, they introduced a range of analytic methods to the federal government, including cost-benefit analysis, operations and systems research, and linear programming.

This office was viewed as an autonomous unit, made up of individuals with well-hewn skills who were not likely to have detailed knowledge of the substance of the policy assignments given them. Their specializations were in the techniques of analysis, not in the details of their application. Though these staff members thought of themselves as specialists, their specializations were not a part of the areas of expertise found within the traditional bureaucracy. As would become clearer as the field developed, these staff members were viewed as individuals who had much more in common with short-term political appointees than with the career public service.

Several other patterns emerged that had a dramatic impact on the field. There was an assumption that the policy analysts who were assem-bled would constitute a small, elite corps, made up of individuals who would be expected to spend only a few years in the federal government.

Most of the individuals hired were trained as economists or operations researchers who had fairly recently received PhDs; a significant number of them came to Washington from RAND, where they had worked on similar assignments in the past. Their frames of reference and support systems were atypical for a federal employee; many brought their past relationships with think tanks, consultants, universities and other analytical organizations with them as they did their work.

Sometimes called the "Whiz Kids," this staff was highly visible; both its PPBS activity and its general expertise came to the attention of President Lyndon Johnson. In October 1965, the Bureau of the Budget issued a directive to all federal departments and agencies, calling on them to establish central analytic offices that would apply the PPBS approach to all their budget submissions (Williams, 1998). Johnson argued that the use of "the most modern methods of program analysis" would "insure a much sounder judgment through more accurate information, pinpointing those things that we ought to do more, spotlighting those things that we ought to do less" (Williams, 1998).

Even during these days, however, there were those who were skeptical about the fit between the PPBS demands and the developing field of policy analysis. In what has become a classic article, Aaron Wildavsky argued in *Public Administration Review* in 1969 that the PPBS system had damaged the prospects of encouraging policy analysis in American national government (Wildavsky, 1969).

Even before the Bureau of the Budget directive to create PPBS systems across the federal government was issued, in 1965 the Office of Economic Opportunity had established a small office that was engaged in the functions of planning and program examination, advice and research management. The office also included the budget function, which, according to Walter Williams, was "clearly subordinate to policy analysis" (Williams, 1998). Following the DoD model, the office was found in the top reaches of the agency, and early directors had the direct ear of the agency head.

The policy analysis office that was established in the Department of Health, Education and Welfare in response to Johnson's directive had clear linkages to the DoD office (Radin, 1991) The office that was created was called the Office of Program Coordination, and its first director, William Gorham, had been one of McNamara's Whiz Kids in DoD. A staff of eight people reported to an assistant secretary, who in turn reported to the undersecretary of the department. The original functions of the small staff were defined in response to the PPBS demands and were linked to a multi-year planning process. The office was renamed the Office of the Assistant Secretary for Planning and Evaluation during the Nixon administration.

Recalling the experience of those early days, Alice Rivlin (who joined the original staff in 1965 as one of two deputies to Gorham) emphasized the environment of change and energy that created incredible demands on this staff (Rivlin, 2015). Lyndon Johnson's agenda for social program change seemed insatiable and unstoppable.

In an environment overwhelmed by the Vietnam War, Johnson's expectations about this new function were seen by many to be unrealistic. Trying to balance guns and butter budget goals (domestic policy development in a wartime economy) was difficult enough inside any bureaucracy but found to be more complicated in the US political structure with shared powers between the executive branch and the legislature. The DoD budget developed through the PPBS framework was not only ignored by Congress but it required the department to develop a traditional budget instead of the PPBS effort.

Despite this, some of the domestic policy departments started to establish their own policy analysis offices and sought to advise their cabinet officials using a range of analytic tools. As Alice Rivlin remembers it, "Both advocates and evaluators were naïve by today's standards. We all thought simple interventions could change lives and evaluation would show clear results quickly. It gradually dawned on all of us that progress was going to be more complicated" (Rivlin, 2015).

Arnold Meltsner was one of the few early writers to give sustained attention to questions involving political feasibility and skills in political analysis. His interviews provide a picture of a process that was unfolding that was much different to what the original practitioners expected. Meltsner sought to move the field to a methodology that allowed for analysis of political feasibility, including the identification of actors, their beliefs and motivations, resources, and the sites of their interactions (Meltsner, 1972). Meltsner's emphasis, however, was on the development of micro-level political skills and did not pay significant attention to partisan and societal value conflicts or to appropriate political strategies that might be attached to the policy analyst's recommendations.

During the early years of the field, there seemed to be an implicit acceptance that policy analysts would be governed by the norms of neutrality and objectivity that were embedded in the analysts' culture (Dror, 1984.) The attributes associated with the task of policy analysis include problem definition, definition of goals, information collection, choosing and applying analytical techniques, devising options or alternatives, and making recommendations. It is assumed that these tasks will be accomplished when analysis is clearly separated from the decision-making process. Historically, the policy analysis function was situated squarely in the formulation stage of the policy process – a stage that was viewed as separate from the adoption phase or the implementation phase. As in the tradition dating from Machiavelli, the policy analyst was the advisor, not the decisionmaker. Yet there was little self-consciousness about the behaviors that were appropriate to achieve the goals of the advising relationship (Benveniste, 1977, p. 20).

The fragmentation of the American political system also provides different opportunities for those who advocate particular positions to raise their concerns. The agenda-setting and adoption stages of the policy process provide the setting for political argument. In contrast to the policy formulation stage, both the agenda-setting and adoption stages are essentially political processes, and political reasoning and argument predominate. Each of these stages defines a client (or clients) and each of these clients has a particular perspective on the issue at hand, including levels of authority and political views on the issue. Analysts cannot insulate themselves from the dynamics of politics, interest groups and deadlines. And the clients of the analysts embodied each of those elements.

By the end of this era, the original view of client defined by formal organizational structure was being challenged because of acknowledgment of the complexity of US authority structures in a shared power system. Few decisionmakers had real authority to act unilaterally.

Era 2. The second era of the policy analysis field began in the 1970s and continued to the end of the twentieth century. Meltsner's 1976 book, *Policy Analysts in the Bureaucracy*, was based on 116 interviews with top-level policy analysts in the US federal government during 1970 and 1971 (Meltsner, 1976). Those interviews indicated that the original concept of the policy analyst role did not capture the complexity that was already developing in the policy analysis world. Meltsner's depiction of the policy analysis function brought him to devise a typology that suggested that analysts did not illustrate a single way in which analysts and clients created a relationship. Meltsner's typology differentiated between four types of analysts: Those who had high political skills, those with low political skills, those with high technical skills and those with low technical skills. While some of these elements were derived from the analyst's personal competencies, he linked the choice of analyst to the specific needs of the client.

While the Meltsner typology and analysis was embraced by a number of policy analysis researchers, few used that framework to explore the reasons and consequences of the work of each of the four types of policy analysts, particularly in the relationship between analysts and their clients. Instead attention focused on the supplier of the analysis, not on those who controlled the demand for it.

Meltsner's analysis noted that the analyst's client is not the same as the client of other professionals. The policy analysts he described served clients who were the users, not usually the beneficiaries of the work of the analysts. His interviews uncovered a range of relationships between clients and analysts; they involved immediate relationships, peripheral relationships, remote relationships and future relationships. Even though his information was gleaned from early days of the profession, he picked up on a growing complexity in the client role and differentiated between formal and informal clients. They could be individuals or also collective clients.

Meltsner's depiction supported the complications that Rivlin predicted. Policy analysts had very different clients to advise. The client for their work was no longer limited to the cabinet secretary. Officials up and down the bureaucracy sought advice from the growing group of policy analysts. Policy analysis found its way into Congress as well as into the range of interest groups in Washington. Given limited budgets, the focus moved from creating new policies to finding ways to implement existing policies more effectively. Evaluation techniques entered the approaches to analysis. The evaluation role brought forward analysts (such as Majone, 1989; Lindblom and Cohen, 1989 and Weiss, 1983) who confronted this complexity head on.

The world that faced the early policy analysts in the federal government was very different from that confronting the policy analyst in the 1990s. That world experienced an increase or proliferation of policy analysis offices and activities in federal agencies, legislative settings, think tanks and interest groups. It also illustrated the process of institutionalizing the policy analysis function and redefining the concept of client in the changed environment. These changes included the growth of evaluation, interest in implementation, and creation of an academic identity.

The years that had elapsed since the policy analysis activity began in the 1960s were characterized by dramatic economic, social and political changes in American society. The environment of possibility and optimism of the early 1960s was replaced by a mood of scarcity and skepticism. Indeed, by the end of the 1960s, the experience of the Vietnam War and demands for equality within society forced many to acknowledge that there were large cleavages among groups within the nation. And as the century began to come to an end, public policy within the United States was distinguished by strong value conflicts and issues.

When it became clear that policy analysis was becoming a part of the decision-making process and language, multiple actors within the policy environment began to use its forms and sometimes its substance. As a result, policy analysis became a field with many voices, approaches and interests. As it matured, the profession took on the structure and culture of American democracy, replacing the quite limited practice found only in the top reaches of government bureaucracies that characterized the early stages.

The impact of these macro level changes was not always obvious to policy analysis practitioners in the government. Perhaps the most direct effect of the modifications was in the range of possibilities for policy change that were before them (Nakamura and Smallwood, 1980). Good ideas often did not translate into implementable practices and the interest in implementation began to emerge. This was particularly problematic during the Great Society administration of Lyndon Johnson when policies dealing with civil rights, welfare, education and health were difficult to put into practice. Soon, however, the agenda for many analysts focused mainly on changes in existing policies, not on the creation of new policies and programs. At this point the overlap between the public administration field and the public policy field became clearer.

Policy analysts did experience other shifts in their world. They began to question whether the policy analysis units would be established only at the top of the organizations, looking to the top executives and senior line staffers as the clients for analysis (Rivlin, 1998). These clients would define the perspective, values and agenda for the analytic activity. Once completed, policy analysis would become an additional resource to decisionmakers and thus contribute to the improvement of policymaking. The focus of the activity was upward, and the separate nature of the policy analysis unit minimized concern about the organizational setting in which the analysis took place. Whether or not these individuals were as influential as they hoped to be, this conceptualization of the role became the point of departure for the field.

By the mid-1970s, policy analysis activities had dramatically increased throughout the structure of federal government agencies. As a result, clients for policy analysis were found all over the federal establishment. Most of the units began in the top reaches of departments or agencies. But as time went on, policy analysis offices appeared throughout federal agency structures, attached to specific program units as well as middle-level structures. As it became clear that the terms of policy discourse would be conducted (at least superficially) in analytic terms, those who had responsibility for subunits within departments or agencies were not willing to allow policy shops attached to the top of the organization to maintain a monopoly on analytic activity. Their creation of their own policy units was often triggered by a reluctance to defer to the central-ized unit in the offices of the secretary or agency head. By the mid-1980s, any respectable program unit had its own policy staff – individuals who were not overwhelmed by the techniques and language of the staff of the original policy units and who could engage in debate with them or even convince them of other ways of approaching issues. Both budget and legislative development processes were the locations of competing policy advice, often packaged in the language and form of policy analysis.

As a result, staffers appeared to become increasingly socialized to the policy cultures and political structures with which they were dealing. Those staffers who stayed in an office for significant periods of their careers became attached to and identified with specific program areas and took on the characteristics of policy area specialists, sometimes serving as the institutional memory within the department (Radin, 1997).

The institutionalization and proliferation of policy analysis through federal departments (not simply at the top of the structure) also con-tributed to changes in the behavior of those in the centralized policy analysis units. Those officials became highly interactive in their dealings with analysts and officials in other parts of the departments. Increasingly, policy development took on the quality of debate or bargaining between policy analysts found in different parts of the agency. In addition, policy analysis staff found they shared an interest in activities performed by other offices; in many ways, staffers behaved more like career bureaucrats than the in-and-out analysts envisioned in the early writings on the field

(Rein and White, 1977). Longevity and specialization combined to create organizational units made up of staff members with commitments to specific policy areas (and sometimes to particular approaches to those policies).

In some of the larger federal agencies, the centralized policy shops grew in size, moving from small, almost intimate work groups to compartmentalized and specialized bureaucracies. Recruitment patterns over the years broadened the methodological approach, and the early reliance on economics was complemented by other approaches. Staff were drawn from political science, public administration, and – increasingly – from the public policy graduate schools.

As a result of the spread of the function, staff implicitly redefined the concept of "client." Though there had always been some tension over the client definition – it could be your boss, the secretary, the president, the society or the profession – the proliferation of the profession made this even more complicated. In part this was understandable as analysts developed predictable relationships with programs and program officials over time. Not only were clients the individuals (or groups) who occupied top-level positions within the organization, but clients for analysis often became those involved in the institutional processes within the agency as well as the maintenance of the organization itself. Institutional processes included the standard operating decision procedures in federal agencies (such as planning, budgeting, regulation drafting and legislative drafting), which are predictable and defined by law, internal decision rules and externally imposed calendars (Nelson, 1989). Organizational maintenance as the "client" for analysis developed in the 1980s as the imperative for some analysts became the survival of the agency and maintenance of its programs.

Analysts, not their clients, became the first-line conduit for policy bargaining. The relationships among policy analysts became even more important by the late 1970s, when the reality of limited resources meant that policy debate was frequently focused on the modification of existing programs, not on the creation of new policies. Analysts were likely to be working on issues where they already had a track record, either in terms of substantive policy approaches or involving relationships with others within the organization. Clients often could predict the outcome of an analysis because the analyst was known to prefer a particular approach to an issue. There are stories told about policy analysts who completed analyses that were ignored by one set of decisionmakers. In more than one case, that work simply went into the bottom drawer of the analyst's desk, and when a new set of decisionmakers arrived, the analyst elicited interest from that new cast of characters and pulled out the analytic work that had been ignored earlier. This process was sometimes called "shopping for clients." The balance of dominance between analysts and clients showed signs of tipping. Analysts saw themselves as the center of the activity and assumed that their advice would be welcomed by their clients.

By the mid-1980s, policy analysis activities across the federal government took on the coloration of the agencies and policy issues with which they worked. The policy office in the Department of Health and Human Services (HHS) had an approach and organizational culture that was distinct from that in the Department of Labor or in the Environmental Protection Agency (EPA). For example, agencies with highly specialized and separate subunits invested more resources in the development of policy analysis activities in those subunits than in the offices in centralized locations. The EPA's responsibilities in water, air and other environmental problems were different enough to make such an approach effective. Some policy offices were organized around substantive policy areas (e.g., HHS had units in health, Social Security, social services, and welfare) while others were created around functional approaches to analysis. For example, the Office of the Assistant Secretary for Policy Development and Research (PDR) – the centralized policy office within the Department of Housing and Urban Development (HUD) – had subunits focused on long-term research, evaluation, short-term evaluation and "quick and dirty" analysis (efforts that responded to the secretary's immediate needs). Other units, such as those found in inspector general's offices, actually performed short-term evaluations (Thompson and Yessian, 1992).

Despite these developments, in many instances the role definitions of the policy analyst continued to be expressed in the language and rhetoric of earlier years. One new policy Deputy Assistant Secretary said that his staff members told him that their role was to advise the secretary – yet when queried further, they admitted that none of them had ever had direct contact with the secretary, and what was perceived to be secretarial advising took place through multiple layers of the bureaucracy. Indeed, some have suggested that policy analysts operate with a set of myths about decisionmakers: Among these are the myths that decisionmakers operate like monarchs and that all decisions made by "big people" are always important (House, 1982, p. 36).

As the policy analysis function proliferated within the federal government, it also spread outside the government to include the variety of actors engaged in the policy process. Aaron Wildavsky described this growth in his characteristically straightforward way:

> It takes one to beat one, if only to counter those who are everywhere else – in the interest groups, the congressional committees, the departments, the universities, the think tanks – ensconced in institutions mandated by law to evaluate everything and accept responsibility for nothing.
>
> (Wildavsky, 1979)

The dynamic that spawned the proliferation of policy units within the bureaucracy similarly stimulated the developments outside the organizations. If the policy discourse would be conducted in the language of analysis, then one needed to have appropriate resources available to engage in that discussion. David Weimer and Aidan Vining's (1992) account of policy analysis as an emerging profession described the variety of organizational settings where policy analysts work – multiple settings in the executive branch of the federal government, the legislative branch, state governments (both executive and legislative organizations, local-level executive agencies, think tanks and policy research organizations, and profit-seeking firms in industries affected by government action) (Weimer and Vining, 1989, pp. 9–12). The policy analysts found in each of these settings engaged in their activity in ways that were quite different from the tasks and role envisioned in the early 1960s. It was clear that different clients emerged with quite different agendas.

According to Michael Malbin, a student of congressional staffs, one could find a discernible increase in interest in policy analysis in the US Congress by the 1970s (Malbin, 1980). Clients thus expanded beyond the executive branch of government to the committees and staffs of Congress (Robinson, 1992, p. 184). Despite the interest in policy analysis, the expectations of legislative institutions seemed to be different from those of executive branch policy analysts.

Carol H. Weiss noted that at least some congressional staffers treat analysts "less as bearers of truth and clarity than as just another interest group beating on the door" (Weiss, 1989, p. 3). But analysts did not always agree with that set of perceptions about their role. She suggested that the structure of Congress does act as a deterrent to the use of analysis – tangled committee jurisdictions, tenure of committee members, shortage of time, the oral tradition, staff fragmentation and, of course, the dynamics of decision-making in a legislative body. Yet she found that analysis is valued as staff on committees bring with them respect for analytic procedures. In addition, members of Congress find that they must be in a position to evaluate the work of others; they must be on top of the analytic work produced by agencies and others and help their bosses avoid surprises.

William Robinson argued that the capacity to anticipate issues is the key to effectiveness of the legislative policy analyst (Robinson, 1989, p. 3). He emphasized the importance of timeliness of work and views policy analysts who do not directly serve on committee staff as brokers between decisionmakers and researchers. Yet the Congressional Research Service (CRS) analysts confronted clients that were congressional committees which contained members with very different agendas (Robinson, 1992, p. 6).

Other observers have noted that policy analysis work is of limited utility when ideology has taken over policy debate. Congressional staff members who were participants in the welfare reform debate in the 1990s have suggested that analysis and research are effective only at the margins; policy debates around "big issues" rarely are impacted by so-called neutral information (or at least information that is not pointedly focused on the values of the decisionmakers). Though the analysts may not have played a major role in crafting the broad dimensions of the welfare reform effort, their work did make a difference in the way that specific details were designed.

As a result of these changes, clients were found in every nook and cranny in the city and increasingly policy analysis became integrated into the decision-making process. Yet it was never clear what criteria would be used to assess the impact of those activities. Analysts began to emerge not only in Washington but many were found in state and local settings. The personal relationship between an organization's top official and a middle-level policy analyst had become tenuous. It was not unusual to find negotiation sessions about policy alternatives including analysts as well as decisionmakers. Often the various players in the negotiation brought their own policy analysts with them. Clients of the analyst were not only decisionmakers attached to specific policies but also those involved in the institutional processes of governing (e.g., planning, budgeting, regulation development, legislative drafting).

Analysts were likely to be people trained as sociologists, political scientists or graduates of the growing number of graduate programs in public policy. The roles and skills they employed were diverse and included political, technical, organizational and issue-specific techniques. Clients seemed to expect their analysts to employ both analytic as well as advocacy roles within a diverse array of organizations, suggesting that they were departing from the earlier image of the economist as an analyst qua analyst. The lines between the two players became increasingly fuzzy.

Era 3. By the beginning of the twenty-first century the policy analysis field moved in even more different directions than it had in its past two eras. Yet the new approaches did not always replace the practices of the two earlier eras and the field itself became much more diverse in both role and use of analytic techniques. While up to that point the field had been largely dominated by both practitioners and academics in the US, there was increasing recognition that globalization was now a reality in both the practice and teaching of policy analysis. New attention was given to the differences between Westminster parliamentary systems and the US shared powers system both in terms of the types of analysts who were involved but also in terms of the clients who were a part of the relationship.

We began to understand that the relative importance of different goals, if not the goals themselves, will vary across regimes and societies. These goals were often embedded in the assumptions and expectations of the relevant client. This was quite different to the model created by the New Public Management advocates who sought to apply perspectives and assumptions from the private sector to the public sector and to move toward a one-size-fits-all approach across the globe. Most obviously, different countries are likely to have different constitutional constraints that must be satisfied in routine policy making. Additionally, analysts working in different countries may argue for different trade-offs among goals because of differences in the societies they are trying to make better. Clients thus are likely to be different as one moves across the globe. They may be asking for different sets of plausible policy alternatives that may require new ways of anticipating goals or trade-offs (Weimer, 2012, p. 4). The diversity of approaches found today across the globe provides a rich environment for comparative analysis of the role of clients and their relationship to diverse types of analysts. Yet this set of issues has been largely unexplored in the policy analysis field.

During this period there are also some more general developments in the policymaking process that are likely to influence client expectations. It appears that there has been an increase in client expectations about analysts playing an advocacy role in the way they frame their work. Advocacy creates several difficult situations. It may increase the tension between the client and the analyst if the two players have very different expectations. Part of this is due to the increase in politicization of so many issues. In addition, clients may push for advocacy of an approach with which the analyst does not agree. Also clients have increasingly framed their understanding of an issue in rather narrow budgetary terms, pushing away analytic methods that move to the substance of a policy intervention.

Thus views about decision-making processes have moved to quite a different approach. The individual client was often framed in the hierarchical decision-making model. In that model, decisions followed the traditional hierarchical structure and thus the assumed client would have authority and power to make a decision. By the end of the twentieth century, however, policy analysts often assumed that decision-making was the result of a bargaining process. Thus the proliferation of analysts and analytic organizations fits nicely into the bargaining relationships between multiple players, most of whom were located somewhere within the governmental structure.

By the first decade of the twenty-first century, another approach was added to the decision-making repertoire: The use of networks. The desires of the client are also complicated by the movement toward decision-making networks. But since a network involves multiple players, it is much more difficult to hone in on the specific needs of those involved in decision-making inside the complex arrangements, particularly when the issues at hand involve global players.

Although networks have captured the interest of scholars in a variety of fields both in the US and abroad, it is not always clear how they operate as a formal decision-making approach. Networks are conceptualized as structures that reach across a range of organizational boundaries and, according to Rhodes, operate as "a cluster or complex of organizations connected to each other by resources dependencies and distinguished from other clusters or complexes by breaks in the structure of resources dependencies" (Rhodes, 1992, p. 2).

These are issues that are embedded in situations where the client for the work of a policy analyst is the network itself. Since the network is not an entity with clear or simple goals, how does the analyst determine the interests of the body when – by design – it contains players drawn from multiple interests and settings? And many of those interests represent substantive policy conflicts. These conflicts can emerge from the combination of public sector and private sector players, representatives of interest groups, multiple public agencies and players from the various nodes of the intergovernmental system. In addition, studies of various networks indicate that the interaction of the network itself is crucial and thus it is difficult to focus on substantive policy outcomes when the process of interaction is so important to its success (McGuire and Agranoff, 2011).

It is difficult to characterize the patterns that have emerged as a result of the globalization of the policy analysis field and which have modified the role of the client and their role in the policy analysis effort. Some countries have actually renamed existing data and planning offices and cast them as policy analysis organizations. In other countries, career staff (usually generalists) who traditionally acted as advisors to the party in power have become the core of the policy analysis enterprise. The demise of the Soviet Union provided the impetus in some nations for an organizational unit that could provide advice on alternatives to previous approaches. In still other settings, policy analysis units have been established within autocratic governments to provide at least a façade of openness and a move toward democracy.

Variation in policy analysis approaches can be attributed to the structure of government (e.g., whether it is a centralized or federal system) or to the historic demands of eliminating colonialism, achieving democracy or responding to the end of the Soviet Union. But if anyone was pushed to come up with those comparisons, they are likely to have emphasized the differences in the political structure between a parliamentary system where the executive branch is viewed as a part of the legislative branch and the shared power institutional design found in the US between legislative, executive and judicial systems. It appears that a number of important attributes found in the early days of policy analysis in the US have parallels to the practice of policy advising that takes place in a parliamentary system.

Conclusion

The original concept of the client of the policy analyst was an individual who has authority and is usually located on the top rungs of a public organization. This was modified in the second generation of the profession. Meltsner's depiction of four types of policy analysts with both political and technical skills did acknowledge different roles played by clients as well as different expectations about the relationship between analysts and clients. But even Meltsner's description seemed to assume that the policy analyst would have a quasi-monopoly role in that advising process. By the end of the twentieth century, the image of the policy analyst as the advisor to the Prince (as in Machiavelli) was replaced by an image of an individual operating (usually in a public organization) along with other policy analysts in both public and non-public organizations.

At least three different generations can be identified in this depiction of the development of the policy analysis field that generated different views and roles of clients. And it is quite likely that another generation will develop in the future. It is not surprising that this field is constantly developing and moving since it operates within a highly turbulent environment. At this writing in the second decade of the twenty-first century, it is clear that impacts of globalization have had a significant impact on the field. And shifts in the type of decision-making also have created challenges for policy analysts since analysts are now clearly in so many nooks and crannies in the decision-making world. Thus it is relevant to look at the work that they do, the skills that they require and the background experience that is relevant to them. A comparative lens that captures developments and changes over time as well as contrasts between political systems provides a way of describing this complex and constantly changing field.

All of this is to indicate that it is important for policy analysts to acknowledge the changes that have occurred in our field. This suggests that we must acknowledge that the relationship between analyst and client is important to examine as well as the methodologies and theories used in the process. It's not clear where that relationship will be in ten or 20 years. But it is clear that clients and their expectations have changed over the more than 50 years of our field. These call out for a serious comparative analysis effort to capture the changes in the role and experience of the decisionmaker-client.

Note

1 This chapter is based on an article by Beryl A. Radin entitled "Policy Analysis and Advising Decisionmakers: Don't Forget the Decisionmaker/Client," in the *Journal of Comparative Policy Analysis: Research and Practice*, 18:3, 290–301, 2016.

2 Clients

A Moving Target

The earliest literature in the US describing the formal policy analysis profession emphasized the role played by the client in defining the relationship between the analyst and the client. And it was not surprising that this individual was expected to be found in the bureaucratic halls of the US federal government. Unlike other professionals, the term "client" was used to define the users and not the beneficiaries of the analytic work (Meltsner, 1976, p. 201). While the historical concept of the "client" reached beyond a governmental bureaucracy, in the past it emphasized individuals found in positions of authority and power in royal, hereditary, religious and other settings.

From the beginning of the professional field – despite its links to systems analysis and other developments in economics – there was a tension between two cultures: The culture of analysis and the culture of politics. Despite the acceptance that analysts would be governed by the norms of neutrality and objectivity, it was clear that clients would raise political issues. As Deborah Stone noted, "Reasoned analysis is necessarily political. It always involves choices to include some things and exclude others and to view the world in a particular way when other visions are possible" (Stone, 1997, p. 375). Thus the presence of the client embedded the political perspective that reflected the world of the decisionmaker.

The initial image of the profession that began in the US Department of Defense in the 1960s defined clients as individuals who were identifiable through their job title and defined responsibilities. The hierarchical structure of the federal bureaucracy and the culture of the military led to an emphasis on the cabinet secretary of DoD as the client. That client was someone who appeared to understand both the culture of analysis as well as the culture of politics. Meltsner quoted one of his informants in *Policy Analysts in the Bureaucracy*, published in 1976, in his chapter entitled "Clients." "He's the man you work for.... He's the man who tells you to proceed with the project or approves your analytical recommendations" (1976, p. 201). Yet Meltsner found that a variety of client-analyst relationships emerged in his interviews. About half of the respondents thought that clients would use an analysis and half did not expect that analysts intended the clients to use the analysis. Interaction between the two was extremely variable and direct relationships between analysts and clients were rare (ibid., p. 203). After a decade or so of functioning, Meltsner found that analysts varied tremendously and were hard to characterize (p. 48). Yet he continued to emphasize the role of the client.

When Arnold Meltsner revised his book in 1986, he included developments that indicated some significant changes had taken place in the issues that were defined by clients. Some of these changes reflected the addition of new types of clients and the interests they brought to the process. While bureaucratic clients continued, he noted that the client field grew to include legislative groups, interest groups and other nongovernmental organizations. Meltsner commented on clients' lack of trust in analysis and noted that when clients "become distrustful of advising, they are likely to cut themselves off from new and fresh sources of information" (Meltsner, 1976, p. 371).

In addition, clients not only emerged as individuals but as institutional processes of governing (planning, budgeting, regulation development, legislative drafting) as well as maintenance of an organization. Increasingly clients were including policy analysis as a part of all the stages of the policy process. The earlier emphasis on the policy formulation stage was expanded to include policy adoption, policy implementation and policy evaluation (Radin, 2013, Chapter 2). In addition, by the end of the twentieth century the field had moved beyond the national level to include clients at state and local government levels. This was particularly important in program areas where implementation authority funded by the national government was within the discretion of state or local agencies. There appeared to be little interest in an activity that was termed "policy analysis" beyond US borders.

As a result, the classic role conflict between a client and an analyst was not only defined in terms of personal roles, expectations and attributes but was linked to the complexity of the policy process and the conflict between administration and politics. At that point it seemed to be an American activity even though it had other antecedents.

Changes in the Twenty-First Century

Many clients of analysts continued to be identified because of their positions as individuals with formal authority who are located on the top rungs of a public organization. But other shifts occurred in the policy world that changed the concept of "client." Increasingly participants in the policymaking world found that the formal hierarchical bureaucratic structure does not always describe the decision-making process in a governmental agency. Shared authority was found to be more common and thus a single individual client did not always have the sole authority to act on analytic advice. Multiple decisionmakers are likely to have a role in such a process and can be seen as legitimate actors in the decision-making process. These actors may involve players across different levels of government who have a legitimate role in the policy process.

In other cases these multiple players move beyond governmental entities to involve nongovernmental agencies who are linked together in networks that may be both formal and informal in nature. Often these networks contain a mixture of actors (both from profit and non-profit groups) with different resources and diverse perspectives on an issue. In these cases it becomes quite difficult to define the perspective of "the client" when the "client" is actually a complex organization where players do not always want to be clear about their goals and expectations and instead like the flexibility that accompanies uncertain relationships. The increase in contracting-out activities that traditionally have been done by government employees brings new players to roles in these networks even though they may not have formal authority.

Several other issues have made the contemporary definition of a client extremely complex. There is frequently a conflict between those who approach the policy process as a substantive activity that highlights the quality of public services and those who see it only as the allocation of budget resources. It is not always clear how a client balances those two imperatives since many government structures try to keep the two functions separate. This proves to be difficult as political polarization has increased through the shifts that occur as a result of elections and staff changes.

In addition, the effects of globalization in many policy areas have complicated both the expectations of the client as well as the capacities of the analyst. Given the growth of global relationships policy participants are likely to be more aware of the activity of multinational organizations and the differences between the participants who emerge from different cultures and structures. These include types of policy issues, diverse relationships between analysts and clients, types of analysis required, time frames, stages of the policy process, structures of policy analysis, the boundaries between policy analysis and management, the relationship between career and political actors, skills required and – perhaps most importantly – the structure of the government.

As a result of these changes, ambiguity about the client's role and expectations has increased. This may be related to the increase in informal processes that mask the certainty that is often attached to formal processes. Analysts search for new ways to enter the system at the same time that the formal hierarchical structures do not encourage paths that provide an opening to enter the formal authority.

Lessons from the Cases

The cases that have been used in this study provide contemporary examples of situations that make the identification of a client in the analytic process difficult. Some cases suggest that even after identification of the client the expectations about that role can be confusing. Some of the cases actually depict the client from the perspective of the analyst while others view the client as the dominant player in the relationship.

Ten areas are illustrated by these cases:[1]

- Moving into a new position
- Searching for a client
- Focus on the policy issues
- Dealing with a network
- Organizational limitations, contracting out
- Baggage from the past
- Political and value conflicts within the organization
- Analyst becomes the client
- Conflicting views about role
- Personal and political values

Moving into a New Position

Both Margaret Trumball and James Williams are midcareer analysts who have assumed new positions in existing public organizations. As a result, it is difficult for them to tune into both the formal and informal messages that come from the individuals who have been designated as their clients. While Trumball's move from the UN headquarters in New York to the European Commission headquarters in Brussels puts her in an organization with 28 members (as compared with 193 members of the UN), she does not know whether the individual named as her client has experience or interest in migration issues. She does not know whether she should deal directly with country representatives of the EU or whether she should be advising her client who would communicate with the country reps. While she knows that migration issues are controversial in the EU, she has no idea whether she should avoid making a single recommendation to the members and instead simply define a range of options.

James Williams is an experienced career public servant who has recently moved from an appointment in the Ministry of Education to a newly created policy analysis unit in the Prime Minister's Office in Great Britain. His position is located in the budget office in the unit and he is charged with developing a research budget for colleges and universities that could be defended in Parliament. The creation of the new policy analysis unit was a result of an election where the Labour Party assumed power through the creation of a coalition government. He knew that an earlier staff in the Prime Minister's Office had created standardized statistical and narrative material for submission to central budget panels for assessment. The process that was used in the past was extremely controversial and led to budget allocation patterns that created political problems for the Labour leadership that was then in power. Williams was not close enough to this issue to be able to assess whether his budget boss has assumptions about the direction he should take. He is puzzled about what he should do.

Searching for a Client

Several of the cases illustrate situations in which the policy analyst is in an environment where it is not clear who to identify as the client. Patrick Nonet spent most of his career as a staff member of the provincial government of Quebec. He was a fairly well-known player in the Canadian policy debate over the adoption of French as one of the two languages throughout the country. His past connection with the Quebec position on bilingual requirements made his past policy positions very visible. He was nearing retirement age and agreed to move to Ottawa to work with a new Prime Minister's Commission on language policy. It was not clear to him whether he should view Prime Minister Trudeau as his client or whether he should assume that the *chair of the commission should be his client. The commission's membership represented a multiplicity of views on the topic. Given his expertise, some of his colleagues advised him to act as his own client.*

James Mason had a somewhat similar problem but was at a different point in his career. He was an African American from North Carolina who had focused on race issues in voting both as a staff member of the Legislative Black Caucus and as an active member of the state NAACP organization. He had worked on the campaign staff of the successful Democratic candidate for governor and was offered a job in the Governor's Office. Recently a panel of federal judges struck down North Carolina's congressional map, arguing that it was unconstitutional because of a partisan gerrymander decision. Mason believed that his next job could provide him with a role in the process but wasn't sure that he would be able to work effectively in the Governor's Office where political pressures were likely to include other issues besides voting. He didn't know whether there might be other options that might be more compatible with his personal values or what these options might be.

It seems obvious that WANG Liping's client is the President of the People's Republic of China. Yet the complexity of the environmental issue – constantly moving from an international perspective to a national and even provincial perspective – suggests that it is difficult to think of the President as a sole client of the analysis. One would hope that the analytic process will educate the multiple players and allow them to proceed in a way that acknowledges the impact of any new action on almost all of them. It is likely that each of the members of the informal advisory group that WANG identified will have difficulty articulating the concerns of their own perspective, let alone the others in the group.

Focusing on a Policy Issue

The clients in the early years of the policy analysis profession tended to be individuals who had generalist responsibilities in their organizations. As such these clients often faced quite disparate policy issues. But as the field became more specialized, both analysts and clients developed specialized knowledge of issue-specific programs.

Colleen Hendricks was committed to urban housing issues, particularly those issues that addressed housing problems faced by low-income residents of New York City. Her job at the New York City Housing Authority had provided her with a client who shared her interests and concerns. After five years in this position she began to question whether the city housing authority was an effective client for her concerns. She saw that a number of programs that might have helped New York City residents were controlled by the New York state government. It did not seem that the problems faced by city residents received adequate attention. She felt that she was at a crossroads. Should she think about changing jobs as a way of changing her client and developing new possibilities for policy change?

Dealing with a Network

The interdependency between multiple programs and actors has increased the creation of either formal or informal structures that reach across a range of organizational boundaries that cross both governmental and non-government lines. While they may all have some interest in a particular policy area, those interests often contain conflicting perspectives, diverse resources, power imbalances and policy barriers.

James Marlin was a long-term US Department of Agriculture staff member who was one of the organizers of the Monday Management Group, a network that brought together career staff from a number of federal agencies that were interested in some aspect of rural development. Although organized around federal staff, non-federal groups that were interested in the future of rural America were also involved. These included national organizations as well as representatives of state councils (whose membership included federal, state and local staff as well as for-profit, non-profit and tribal organizations). The boundaries of the interests of the participants expanded over the years without much formalization and it was difficult to describe the aggregate group as a client.

Even though the participants were committed to the process, there really was no way to devise a clear definition of the group's interests. Marlin was also concerned about the permanency of the effort since it never tried to formalize its role or define specific interests beyond its commitment to meet and exchange experiences. His instinct was that formalization would destroy its ability to serve as an effective client.

Dealing with Contracting Out

Hiring a consulting firm to perform an analysis can create a complicated set of expectations regarding the designation of the client in a policy analysis setting. The formal contract that is signed by an agency with either a for-profit or non-profit organization may establish expectations that don't always meet a changing situation.

Renee Hernandez was hired by a consulting firm in Dallas that had a contract to perform policy analysis for the Dallas School District. The analysis specified in the contract drew on the firm's past work using test schools and aggregate data to assess the performance of individual schools. This was Hernandez's first job after completing her public policy master's degree at the LBJ School at the University of Texas at Austin. During her academic program she had focused on performance assessment of schools in Texas with large bilingual student populations. She had grown up in the Rio Grande Valley and started school speaking only Spanish.

After several months in the role, she noticed that there was more attention given to the performance of African American students than to Hispanic students. Although a new superintendent had been recently hired by the school system, that individual continued an evaluation system that used performance and student results to measure principal and teacher effectiveness. That information was being used to determine which schools should be closed.

Hernandez realized that the formal contract signed by both her employer and the school district was likely to define the client for her work. She was increasingly concerned that this work would not address the changing needs of the school system but did not know how to deal with that confusing situation.

Baggage from the Past

We tend to think of clients as individuals who have expertise in a policy area. But not all clients are individuals who come to their positions with previous knowledge of the constraints associated with their current position. Unlike career staff, political appointees are often people who have policy expertise that is obtained in nongovernmental settings.

Jonathan Weston was appointed to a position in the US Department of Energy because of his visibility as the chairman of a Government Affairs Committee of the Association of Windmill Manufacturers. He was well known in both the executive branch and Congress as he had closely monitored existing legislation involving windmills. In that role he was concerned about competition from windmill companies in other countries but also had focused on what he saw as a regulatory burden on his constituency.

His appointment sailed through the system and the policy analysis staff assigned to work for him had learned to anticipate the questions that he had about their analytic work. When he started the job, he assumed that it would be relatively easy to transfer his experience from the private sector to the public sector since he knew what was likely to occur in the "real world." After several months he began to realize that his new role required him to look at issues that were unfamiliar to him. His analytic staff raised concerns (such as budget allocations) that involved other agencies and issues that seemed to be unique to the public sector. These realizations not only surprised him but also confused the analysts who reported to him.

James Williamson was recently hired by a consortium of foundations that supported higher education programs for low-income students. The consortium is 20 years old and is composed of seven different foundations that provide resources to approximately 12 higher education public agencies across the US. While new to this job, Williamson was quite familiar with its activities since in the past he had been employed by two of the state agencies that received funds from the consortium. Although both states attempted to reach similar goals, he was struck by the differences between them in terms of their past experiences, the pathways they took to achieve the same goals, and their relationship with the consortium.

Williamson's past experiences in those two states made him sensitive to differences between the two settings. But he also knew that his new job required him to define clear expectations about the use of the consortium's funding. There was pressure within the organization (largely through its board) to establish a single model of expectations that imposed a clear model of success on the program. He realized that despite his familiarity with the program there were two quite different clients for his work. One was the board that was composed of representatives of each of the seven funders while the other was the state programs who would implement the program.

Political and Value Conflicts within the Organization

It is not uncommon for clients in an organization to change as a result of elections, reorganizations or simply change of staff. In other instances, organizations often have to balance conflicting roles and perspectives that create different forms of instability.

Marjorie Benson entered the US government through a fellowship available to graduates of public policy programs. Her interests during graduate school focused on health issues and she spent all of the eight years of the Obama administration in the Office of the Assistant Secretary for Planning and Evaluation in the Department of Health and Human Services working on the development of the Affordable Care Act.

At the end of the Obama administration she took maternity leave for a year. When she returned to the federal government she joined a staff that had new political leadership that was committed to ending the ACA. Her client was *someone who had been a member of the Republican staff of the House Ways and Means Committee and was committed to the demise of the ACA. She found the situation very difficult and didn't know what alternatives might be available to her.*

Ellen Winston knew she wanted to organize her career around welfare policy issues. When she completed her MPP degree she was able to choose between three different non-profit organizations that focused on welfare issues. She chose the one that had a separate organizational unit that did analysis and research. After a year on the job she realized that both the policy analysis office as well as the lobbying office reported to the same vice president in the organization who tried to blend staff who used both approaches. Winston found that the lobbyists on the staff were committed to alternatives that would generate support in Congress, in state and local settings, and in other lobbying organizations. By contrast, she and the policy analysis staff saw the mission as furthering knowledge in the field. That perspective rarely seemed to prevail. The research orientation was constrained by limits of resources, time and support and she thought that the lobbyists had really become the client for the analytic staff.

The Analyst Becomes the Client

Despite the acknowledgment that the role of the client is quite different from that of the analyst, there are instances when the two roles become very difficult to separate. This may occur in the later stages of an analyst's career when an individual's reputation and experience makes it difficult to separate these two roles.

Joyce Winter is a well-known policy analyst dealing with environmental issues in California. She has had a range of positions in both the state and federal governments and has worked with a number of environmental public interest groups. She is recognized as an important player in the development of California's leadership role in the environmental field. By the second year of the Trump administration it became clear that the conflict between California and the federal government's environmental policies was a reality. Winter felt that it was important for her to deal with that conflict by organizing the California players in an umbrella organization that took advantage of their experience and concerns. She realized that no such organization was in existence and decided that it was time for her to create such an organization. She knew that her role would not be a typical policy analyst role but more like that of a client.

Reema Chatterjee had been working for the International Monetary Fund (IMF) on projects dealing with infrastructure developments for the past 25 years. She was based in Washington but spent more than half of her time traveling to projects in a range of countries around the globe. She had originally arrived in the US to complete a PhD in economics as a member of the Indian Administrative Service and decided to apply for a position at the IMF. She stayed there, married another Indian who worked at the World Bank, purchased a home in the Washington suburbs and had two children who attended American schools and identified as Americans.

Both Chatterjee and her husband learned that they were eligible for generous lifetime pensions from their organizations and decided that this support would allow them to live in Delhi and spend time with their Indian families. Neither of them had considered that the India they knew from the past had changed quite dramatically. They had planned to develop a consulting organization but were not sure whether that was possible given the changes in the country. They realized that the new situation required them to move beyond their familiar analytical role and find some way to create work that would help them develop clients.

Conflicting Views

Many of the issues that become a part of the analyst's agenda arise from strong and diverse views within an organization that are expressed by two or more clients. An analyst's choice between those different views can create serious problems for both sets of actors.

Marianne Williams has completed three years working for the Baltimore Police Department on their Performance-Stat effort. That assignment was attached to the desire of the Mayor of Baltimore to assure that the police department was meeting the expectations of the Mayor and the city council. By the second year of her assignment she began to see differences in performance by police staff located in different parts of the city. The data she was collecting was organized on a city-wide basis and did not differentiate between differences across the city that might have resulted from diverse populations and very different settings. The death of Freddie Gray – an African American who died in police custody – became a focusing event in the city and seemed to support views about those differences. Although her official assignment was to continue to collect information on a city-wide basis, she did not see a way to change that approach. She did not think she had a way to shift her client from accountability to the Mayor to the low-income residents of the city and to generate resources to make that happen.

Curtis Brown has been given an important assignment by the Director of the Virginia Department of Corrections He has been asked to develop a strategy that would result in the addition of new prisons to the department's structure. This assignment emerged as a result of a pending legal case brought by prison advocacy groups alleging prison overcrowding. If the court continues to move on the case, the Director of the Department is likely to lose control over the issue. He is also concerned that the department does not have the resources to deal with the issue despite the extensive public reaction to the effects of overcrowding. In addition, almost all of those reactions called for building a new prison in urban northern Virginia even though most of the current state prisons are in rural areas.

Brown is aware that there are at least two different views about the situation. One group of individuals argues that this project provides an opportunity for the department to contract its design and management to the private sector and bring a group of contractors to this issue. By contrast, another group in the department believes that the facility should be controlled by the department and kept inside the current system where the department would design and manage the new prison. Brown is skeptical that it would be possible to devise a solution that combines both approaches (effectively making advocates of both his potential clients). He is being pressured to make a clear choice between the two strategies.

Personal Values

It is not unusual for policy analysts – especially younger individuals whose personal values and experiences seem to collide with their work assignments – to find themselves in uncomfortable situations with their clients. Sometimes those clients are implicit rather than explicit but both types make job responsibilities difficult.

George Smith was the first person in his West Virginia family to complete a masters' degree at a university. His public policy degree made him the first male member of his family who was not working in a coal mine by the time he reached voting age. His grandfather had been one of the top officials in the mine workers' union and had been involved in creating the mine workers' health system that provided medical services to mining families.

During the 2016 presidential election Smith found it difficult to listen to those who argued that the coal mining industry was dying. But he was also aware that the promises that were made about reinvigorating the coal industry were not realistic. Smith was concerned that many West Virginia residents were not able to think realistically about future development in the state.

Younger people were leaving the state largely because educational opportunities were not available to them. Fewer and fewer of his childhood friends were living in the state. Smith was attempting to devise a job search that would allow him to live with his personal values, be realistic about a job, and use his academic training. He wasn't sure whether that was possible.

Conclusion

These examples indicate that defining and dealing with clients continues to be very important in the contemporary world of policy analysis. At the same time, the behaviors and role of the client now make up a very diverse sets of practices and experiences. Clients have moved far from the policy analysis relationships of the 1960s which were limited to a bond between a cabinet secretary and an economist who served as the analyst in the relationship. Both clients and analysts are found in many nicks and crannies around the globe, in both public and private settings, and with very diverse expectations about what will emerge from their role. As will be discussed in Chapter 3 (focusing on the analyst), the relationship between clients and analysts continues to be an ever-changing yet essential factor in this field.

Note

1 There are many other situations that involve the role of the client but these ten issues provide representative examples.

3 The Analyst
Expectations and Constraints

The definition super has grown broad

For more than 50 years both academics and practitioners have tried to find a way to define the field that we call policy analysis. Unlike fields such as economics, political science, public management or sociology it has been more difficult to agree on the intellectual location of the field or what it actually accomplishes. When I tried to explain "policy analysis" to family members one of my relatives was convinced it defined a person who examined insurance policies.

Although the field of policy analysis had its original roots in the world of decision-making and practice, its development over a half century has created an academic field that is located around the globe. It is found in many different institutions of higher education, is the main subject of a number of journals and other publications, the focus of national and international organizations, and continues to generate debate about the parameters of its research subjects and methodologies. Examination of articles in what are viewed as policy journals uncovers a wide range of methods and approaches to the topic. But most of the literature focuses on the analytical techniques employed by the analyst and not on the process of interacting with the client.

There is also a lack of clarity about its dimensions as a part of the field of practice. Jobs with the label "policy analyst" can be found but they are often subsections of jobs in the category of program or budget analyst. While the early years of the field assumed that "policy analysts" were always found in bureaucratic government jobs, current job advertisements suggest that positions in the field are also found in a wide range of non-profit and for-profit settings as well as in legislative organizations. In some cases, while jobs are called "policy analyst" positions, the employment requirements suggest that organizations are looking for staff who might be more accurately defined as "policy advocates" rather than "policy analysts."

As the cases used in this volume suggest, there is not a single definition of the term "policy analyst" that would be agreed to by the players in either the academic or practitioner settings. The early years of the field that began in the US Department of Defense in the 1960s appeared to indicate a setting that may have given the original policy analysts an illusion of agreement on the definition of the job. During those early years it seems to have been possible to reach agreement that the early clients of the new process were high-level officials in the government who sought advice on the development of new policies. And the clients were often familiar with the analytic techniques that the analysts were using.

Similarly, it was possible to attain agreement on the role and background of those who were then defined as policy analysts. They were economists who were likely to have a specialty in systems analysis and were likely to draw on their skills in benefit-cost analysis. They were familiar with the Program Planning Budgeting System (PPBS), the decision allocation process that allowed them to link planning and program analysis to the budget process. The original group was composed of individuals who had worked for the RAND Corporation in Santa Monica, California on defense-related issues. Some of them saw their careers as in-and-out consultants while others expected to craft a career around their government service. Many of them seemed confident that the analytical approaches used in Defense would be effective in other federal agencies and applicable to other policy problems and issues.

This sense of optimism also reflected the views of the Kennedy administration. The "New Frontier" had attracted a group of experts to the shores of the Potomac who saw the possibilities in the new activity. Although this optimism was challenged by the assassination of John Kennedy and the attention to the war in Vietnam, Lyndon Johnson was especially intrigued by the possibilities raised by these Department of Defense experts and chose to require that it be used throughout the government. Those expectations were rarely met.

Arnold Meltsner, the author of *Policy Analysts in the Bureaucracy*, and a former staffer at RAND, moved to the faculty at the University of California at Berkeley when the Graduate School of Public Policy (now the Goldman School) was created. In 1976 Meltsner became the first academic to attempt to capture the work, views and limitations of the individuals who were then being called "policy analysts" (Meltsner, 1976, p. 4). In many ways his interviews with these individuals emphasized their unique qualities. He wrote about the impact of their training, their formal education, beliefs about reality, and motivations to make an impact on policymaking. He distinguished between analysts who were technicians, politicians, or entrepreneurs and emphasized that policy analysts often set their own expectations (ibid.).

As it developed, the field itself was experiencing growing pains and the definition of success in the practice of policy analysis was not always obvious or agreed upon. Several questions were difficult to answer. Was success the ability to convince the client/decisionmaker to adopt your recommendation? Was an analyst successful when he or she helped the client understand the complexity and dimensions of a policy choice? Was the analyst successful when the work performed was publishable and approved by one's peers within the profession? The norms behind each of these questions suggested that policy analysis was a field that embraced the values of science, neutrality and research at the same time it also embraced pragmatic values of utility.

As the years went by, the field did seem to be moving toward a professional identity for policy analysts. Schools and departments of public policy spread across the country. Some were free standing while others were parts of public administration, political science or business programs. Some academic programs were known for their interest in specific policy areas and joint degree programs became more common. A professional organization (the Association of Public Policy Analysis and Management) was created and yearly research conferences were held that provided an opportunity for both academics and practitioners to present their findings. Curricula requirements and subject offerings tended to move in similar directions; MPP (Masters in Public Policy) programs usually had quantitative analysis requirements, policy process courses and applied projects that emphasized application rather than theory. Faculty tended to come from more traditional academic fields and in the early years many of them came to the academy with practitioner experience in the growing policy analysis field. However, as the programs proliferated fewer faculty had practitioner experience before coming to the academy.

But at the same time, many issues remained unresolved or at least unclear. Both efforts labeled as policy analysis and those called fiscal decision-making seemed to be important but the two approaches continued to have an uneasy relationship. Analysts were usually located in organizational units attached to the highest levels of a department or

Silloed Thinkers + implimeness makes real suggestions hard

agency and found themselves separated from staff units charged with operating responsibilities. That was particularly difficult when policy analysts were focusing on implementation alternatives and strategies.

Conflicting advice emanated from Meltsner and from Israeli political scientist Yehezkel Dror. Dror called for broadening the scope of the analyst's role beyond the use of technical skills to encompass the organizational and political realities that made up "the public interest" (Dror 1971, quoted in Radin, 2013, pp. 26–7). It was not easy to calculate "the public interest" in the diverse and fragmented American society but, despite that, policy analysts grew in numbers and visibility. They showed up in middle and lower levels in the bureaucracy and became increasingly socialized to the policy cultures and political structures in which they were dealing.

By the end of the twentieth century, the list of skill areas that were thought to be relevant to a skilled policy analyst had become more extensive. Meltsner's dichotomy between technical skills and political skills was relatively simple. The technical skills he found had emerged from economics and systems analysis and the political skills emphasized the realities faced by the relevant clients. The newer group of skills reached beyond those used in the search for the formulation and adoption of new policies and moved into the implementation and evaluation stages of the policy process that often included existing policies and programs. Thus the practice was likely to include the following skills (Radin, 2013, p. 164):

- Case study methods
- Cost-benefit analysis
- Ethical analysis
- Evaluation
- Futures analysis
- Historical analysis
- Implementation analysis
- Interviewing
- Legal analysis
- Microeconomics
- Negotiation, mediation
- Operations research
- Organizational analysis
- Political feasibility analysis
- Public speaking

- Small-group facilitation
- Specific program knowledge
- Statistics
- Survey research methods
- Systems analysis

(Radin, 2013, 164–5)

Analysis vs. Research

By the early years of the twenty-first century, Vining and Weimer provided an alternative definition of policy analysis that moved beyond the earlier definitions offered by Meltsner and Dror. It required both a client and a substantive focus on advancing social values. They wrote:

> We distinguish it [policy analysis] from policy research, which shares the substantive focus but not the requirement of a specific client, and from political/organizational, or stakeholder, analysis, which has a specific client but an instrumental rather than substantive focus.... We recognize policy process as distinct from, but nevertheless, potentially informative for political/organizational and policy analysis.
>
> ("The Foundations of Public Administration: Policy Analysis,"
> Public Administration Review, ASPA, 2010)

Yet few of the academic programs that identified themselves as "public policy schools" agreed with the Vining-Weimer differentiation between research and analysis. More were likely to fudge the differences between the two approaches and could not define themselves within only one of the quartiles of the table that Vining and Weimer included in their article (See Table 3.1). While Vining and Weimer argued that there was significant difference between the client focus attached to policy analysis and the academic/societal focus that defined the policy research approach, that differentiation is not always acknowledged within the community of people who call themselves policy analysts.

For some analysts, the responsibilities attached to the relationship with a client seemed to be a departure from the values of objectivity and neutrality built into the research role. It opened the door to conceptualizing their role as an advocate but with values embedded in the analyst's personal perspective.

Table 3.1 Taxonomy of "Policy Analysis"

		Client Versus Societal Focus	
		Client Focus	Academic/Societal Focus
Substantive versus process focus	Substantive policy/policy analytic focus	Policy Analysis (narrowly defined) Problem-solving focus Economics pre-eminent Comprehensive: Problem analysis (market and government failure), synthesis, solution analysis (alternatives, goals, assessment) Goals clear, or at least emergently clear; efficiency (cost-benefit) or efficiency, equity, government revenue-expenditure (multi-goal)	Policy Research/Policy Sciences Social science research on policy problems Policy problem discovery/exploration Solution (policy) discovery/exploration Broad range of social sciences, but economics, political science dominate Partial or fragmentary (in terms of policy problem) Goals contestable
	Policy process focus	Political/Organizational Analysis (or Stakeholder Analysis) Political, organizational, and inter-organizational analysis (including networks) Relevant for both adoption and implementation Strategic client focus Often informal and unwritten Primarily descriptive and predictive, rather than normative: Goal is adoption and implementation	Policy Process Research All social science research, but dominated by political science research Distributional and re-distributional focus (iron triangles, etc.) Theory somewhat contestable: interest group theory, advocacy coalition, path dependency, etc, but converging on contingent and comprehensive theory

Source: Vining and Weimer, 2010.

As a result, the term "policy analyst" continues to confuse many people in academic programs (both faculty and students) as well as in the world of practice. Most of the individuals who are viewed as "analysts" in the cases that are used in this volume represent quite different examples of the typology proposed by Vining and Weimer. Just as clients/decisionmakers come to their role wearing very different clothing with diverse expectations about their use of analytic work, analysts also differ in terms of their expectations.

While the Vining and Weimer taxonomy is very useful, it does ignore another element in conceptualizing the role of the policy analyst. The cases that are used in this analysis indicate that there is a complicated relationship between the analyst's personal values and expectations and those embedded in the position itself.

Conflict between an Analyst's Personal Values and the Position Itself

Nearly all of the cases used in this analysis provide evidence of various levels of conflict between the analyst's personal values and past experience and the expectations of the position they find themselves in. This conflict often makes it difficult to both approach the issue at hand and to make a recommendation. Here are some examples:

Margaret Trumball in the European Commission headquarters faces an issue that she believes to be intractable and incredibly conflictual. That issue is immigration policy. Given her past experience, she believes that it is not possible to present a recommendation to the incredibly diverse groups who are her clients because of this situation. She thinks it makes more sense to give them the possible alternatives that have emerged from her analysis. She is also fearful of being labeled an advocate for a single approach.

James Williams in the Prime Minister's Office in Great Britain is confronted with a policy issue that has a difficult political history. The previous decision regarding the allocation of research funds to colleges and universities was based on an allocation process that ignored teaching criteria and thus violated the values of the academy. It is believed that this past decision led to the end of the Labour government. Labour is now in power but is part of a coalition government. Thus his client is vulnerable no matter what Wilson (1989) recommends. He is trying to figure out an alternative to the past experience but feels that he is likely to repeat the problems of the past.

Marjorie Benson is on the health staff of the Office of the Assistant Secretary for Policy and Evaluation of the US Department of Health and Human Services. She was on maternity leave when the administration changed and is having a difficult time working with her current boss who opposes the Affordable Care Act. Her commitment to that Act (which was passed during the Obama administration) is personal and very strong. She is trying to figure out how to survive in the new environment in a way that allows her to be true to her values. It's not clear what alternatives (including quitting her job) make sense for her to consider.

James Marlin is a long-time staff member in the US Department of Agriculture who is approaching retirement. Over the years he was one of the few people in the department who organized an informal group of federal officials from many departments who were concerned about rural policy issues. The group – effectively a network – was viewed as extremely effective both in Washington and in the state rural development programs. He was able to do this without taking any formal action. The effort did not have a budget, any legal authority, a formal structure or involvement with Congress. He is trying to figure out how to continue these efforts after his retirement. He believes that the success that the network achieved grew directly out of its informal nature but he doesn't know what alternatives are available to him.

Patrick Nonet has been working for the Canadian province of Quebec and is known as an advocate for the bilingual approach of including both English and French as official languages of Canada. He is approaching retirement and has taken a position on the staff of a Prime Minister's Commission that will examine the future of the existing language policy. The position is in Ottawa, the national capital of Canada. He understands the economic rationale for a change of the expensive policy especially since a significant percentage of French speakers are now comfortable with English. But he is very sensitive to the symbolism of the past requirements since it was a major acknowledgment that two separate cultures exist in the country. He finds it difficult to trade-off between economic and symbolic issues given his past commitment to the language policy.

Joyce Winter is a well-known policy analyst dealing with environmental issues in California. She has worked in both state and federal organizations and has been an environmental advocate for many years. She is very familiar with the arguments made by scientists that supported the Obama policies. The current conflict between California and the federal government makes her feel that she needs to use her expertise to produce policy documents in this environment. In addition, she knows that Governor Jerry Brown will soon leave office and she wants to build on his influence and role. She is trying to determine whether she should organize an organization to support her positions and make it clear that she is a policy advocate.

Renee Hernandez is a new policy analyst working for the Dallas School District through a contract between the district and a local consulting firm. The district has a diverse student body, composed of Hispanics, African Americans and Anglos. Her assignment has been to work on the evaluation system put in place by the past Superintendent of Schools and supported by the Board of Education. She has noticed that the current system is attentive only to issues faced by African American students. Her cultural background as a Hispanic has made her very uncomfortable with the situation. There is a conflict between the assignment she was given by the consulting firm and what she is seeing as she attends school board meetings and examines the past work performed by her employer. She doesn't know what to do.

Marianne Williams is also facing a disjuncture between her job assignment in the Baltimore Police Department and the world that she sees when she moves around the city. She had been hired to continue the Performance-Stat process that was nationally hailed as an effective performance measurement effort. But the death of Freddie Gray and the riots in the African American community in Baltimore that followed showed her that the analytic process they employed did not provide information that could help the city respond to this crisis. She'd like to continue to work in Baltimore but is concerned that many jobs shared the limitations of the performance measurement process.

James Mason is a native North Carolinian who is looking for a job. He has worked on political campaigns in the state and has been active in the state NAACP organization. A recent legal decision by a panel of federal judges ruled that the current North Carolina congressional map is unconstitutional. He is looking for a job that would allow him to support this ruling but he doesn't know whether such a job exists. He believes that his past experience makes him an effective advocate for the legal decision.

George Smith also has a strong identity with his personal roots. He feels that recent attempts to eliminate the coal industry in West Virginia are an implicit criticism of his family's history in the coal miners' union. Yet he knows that attempts to find ways to allow the survival of the coal industry are probably unrealistic. He, too, needs a job and wants to stay in the state but cannot figure out how to deal with his personal conflict.

Ellen Winston is committed to working on welfare policy issues. After finishing her MPP and an internship she sought a position in one of the welfare advocacy organizations. She chose an organization that had a separate policy *analysis unit that developed reports and research efforts on topical issues. She felt that this staff added credibility to advocacy work by grounding it in evidence. After a few months she realized that both the policy analysis unit and the lobbying office reported to the same vice president. It was clear to her that the positions of the lobbying office almost always became the policies of the organization even if the policy analysis unit had differences with them. She found that the organization was more concerned about political realities and a short time frame than research. Her commitment to research has made her very uncomfortable with her position.*

Colleen Hendricks had a somewhat similar problem. Her commitment to improving housing policy for low-income New Yorkers was more important to her than loyalty to her current city organization. As a result, she is seriously thinking of changing jobs, moving from a job in the local government to one in the state government. She believes that the state government has control over funds (especially federal funds) that might be distributed to the city. She is uncertain about such a move and fearful that she can be effective in a different environment.

Veronica Lopez is a well-known physician who has moved from clinical positions to both national and international health policy organizations. Her current position at the World Health Organization is unusual since she is both an insider and an outsider to the organization. She has been able to operate in very diverse settings and play a boundary spanning role with policy participants who have quite different perceptions of different health policy issues.

Other Patterns That Emerge from the Cases

In addition to the issues related to values, there are also other patterns that emerge from the cases. These include: The stage of an analyst's career, their training background, their current organizational setting, their future career plans, their relationship with the client, defining the policy problems, and expectations about the approach (use of technical vs. political skills).

Stage of an analyst's career. The 16 examples of policy analysts are distributed fairly equally between three categories: (1) individuals who are at the early stages of their career, (2) midcareer people, and (3) people anticipating retirement. Despite the differences in the location of their job and the subject of their policy work, the stage of career appears to generate particular forms of behavior. The younger analysts are often worried about keeping a job in a difficult employment situation. Many midcareer staff seem to be committed to a policy area. And senior staff appear to be concerned about "making a difference." It appears that specific career expectations are built into a number of the cases in all three groups.

Training background. In only about a third of the cases did analysts have specialized training in policy analysis (largely at graduate level). That training usually included courses in analytic techniques but few of the cases indicated make use of those techniques. Others had other forms of specialized training including international management and development, public management, generic management skills (such as budgeting) and a range of substantive policy areas (including rural issues, environment, social welfare, housing and criminal justice.)

Current organizational setting. Many of the cases involved analysts who were working in a government agency. In a few cases, the analyst came to the task from experience and a perspective outside of the agency. As such they are both inside and outside of the government organization. A few cases involved people who were looking for a job or considering looking for a new job because of discomfort with their current experience. Most were in a US agency but distributed in national, state and local settings. Local settings were specialized bureaucracies (e.g., welfare, education, housing, criminal justice) and, in one case, a state agency. Two people were in the bureaucracies of other countries and two in international organizations that were new to them (and one had left such an organization). One person worked for a non-profit organization and one worked for a consulting firm. Most of the settings had their own clear cultures with cultures that were not always consistent with analysts' expectations.

Future career plans. Most of the individuals seemed to have a commitment to a specific policy area while a few saw their career moving within their current organization. It is not clear whether these individuals expected to play the same role they played in their current job in the future. Neither was it clear that they saw themselves moving to other parts of the agency (e.g., the budget office or the part of the agency actually delivering the services).

Relationship with the client. Almost all of the analysts in the cases experienced uneasy relationships with their clients. About a third of them had problems because of a clash of values with the client or the client's organization while about two-thirds of them had difficulty figuring out the expectations of the client. These problems emerged from the complexity of the organization, the multiplicity of perspectives within the client role, and the changes that were occurring in the organization. Political changes often brought policy shifts that emphasized this complexity. One case that was written from the perspective of the client illustrated his experience learning from the analysts on his staff (this is sometimes called "educating the client"). In several cases the client and analyst roles were difficult to disentangle.

Defining the policy problem. The cases indicated that analysts had quite diverse experiences defining the policy problem they were expected to analyze. About a third of the cases indicated that analysts received clear expectations and definitions of the problem. Another third seemed to have semi clear or partial expectations provided. The last third were given definitions of the problem that contained conflictual expectations, a number of which emerged from multiple clients who represented conflicting views within the policy area.

Expectations about approach: Technical or political? In a few cases, analysts were told what analytic approach they would employ in their assignment (both of the examples involved performance measurement techniques). The approach was determined by the client and the analyst had no real role that allowed them to question that decision. In other cases the analysis was tied to the politics of the existing budget process or to more explicit political pressures.

Conclusions

This discussion of policy analysts indicates that the field of practice of policy analysts has become much more diverse and complex than the assumptions made about those who were the early practitioners of the new profession. The analysts in the cases that have been analyzed in this chapter do share some basic similarities with their "ancestors." They are faced with a wide range of policy problems and are expected to give advice to an actor (or actors) who look for answers to these problems. But the analysts today continue to confront uncertain criteria that would provide them with a definition of success.

As this discussion has indicated, analysts today are frequently unable to take comfort in the application of formal analytic techniques to the policy problem before them. In part, this conflict emerges from the reality that analysts are often playing the role of an advocate rather than a traditional analyst who is advising the client and putting their own

advocate   or   advisor ?

values in check. In that sense, today's analysts continue to measure their success in some of the ways that their predecessors did. They believe they are successful if their client adopts the recommendation they have made. Sometimes they believe they are successful when they educate the client and help them understand the complexity of a policy choice. Some measure their success in terms of producing work that is publishable or presented in a professional setting. But that, as Vining and Weimer have argued, is a measure of success that is more relevant to those whose work is research.

In addition, success is also different for analysts who are at different stages of their career. Those who are in their early stages are thinking about their next position and many of them seek their next jobs as advocates for policy changes that emerge from their personal values. Mid-career analysts are often also identified with policy changes but rest on the expertise they have in an area. And analysts who are approaching retirement are attempting to find a way to contribute their knowledge to future policymakers and, as such, seem to combine the role of analyst with that of the client.

1. Client adopts rec
2. educate client
3. produce publishable work.

4   The Policy Environment

Increasing Acknowledgment of Complexity

The early literature in the field seems to suggest that both analysts and clients did not spend much time or energy thinking about the dimensions of the policy environment in which they worked. If they had been asked to develop a conceptual map of the players and functions involved in the policy analysis process it would have been very straight forward. Two elements seem to have been assumed. The first was that the centerpiece of the effort was the personal relationship between the analyst and the decisionmaker, often the cabinet secretary or another high-ranking individual in a bureaucracy. While there were likely to be conversations between the cabinet secretary and players in the White House, it seemed to be quite rare for the analyst to focus on the substantive impact of those relationships. Each of the cabinet secretaries was expected to operate autonomously and policy overlaps were rarely assumed.

At that early point in the development of the policy analysis field there was little attention given to the political structure in which the advising process took place. Indeed, the focus was on that personal relationship between the analyst and the decisionmaker being advised. In some ways, the ancient and traditional views about advisor and decisionmaker seemed to be relevant. As Goldhamer (1978, p. 3) wrote, "the adviser is generally one whose advice has been proffered to the supreme leader of a nation." Few of the historical advisors operated in a political system that approximated a democracy. And as became clearer in the future, the differences between a political system devised as a parliamentary structure (e.g., the United Kingdom) and that devised as a shared power system (the US) did not receive much attention.

The second element stemmed from the location of the early efforts: The US Department of Defense (DoD). DoD was a military organization that took the formal hierarchical structure of government quite seriously. That structure defined the relationships between top officials and lower level staff as well as a relatively clear differentiation between the organization and those outside of it. There was minimal attention to the informal relationships within government and between government and the actors outside of its borders. There was a tendency to look only at the substantive policy as if it operated in a cage by itself. That meant that the early analysts seem to have minimized the role of organizational processes surrounding the formal substantive policy decisions. While early policy analysis was linked to the federal budget process, other decision processes such as regulatory decisions, the impact of the policy on existing policies within the organization, and the substantive impact of the policy on those outside the organization were largely ignored.

In addition, it did not seem that analysts who were creating the new profession focused on the role of congressional players in the decision process. In fact, DoD agencies tended to develop two separate budgets – one for the Secretary and the White House and a different one for Congress. At that time, DoD tended to rely on their historical support from members of Congress as long as the budget benefits of programs continued to be distributed around the country to them.

The early analysts focused almost exclusively on the formulation stage of the policy process. That meant that recommendations were more likely to create brand new programs and policies and did not require a lot of attention to existing programs and staff within the department. Both clients and analysts were future oriented and rarely looked at those involved in past efforts.

The differences in role between the original analysts and their clients seemed to be quite clear. The technical abilities of the analysts were emphasized and expected to serve the needs of the clients. But when Meltsner published *Policy Analysts in the Bureaucracy* in 1976, he did acknowledge that analysts varied in terms of skill and interests. He differentiated between technicians and politicians but interestingly thought of politicians as bureaucrats and generalists who were "just as likely to serve themselves as they are to serve the secretary" (Meltsner, 1976, p. 31). He noted that they "want to be where the action is" (Meltsner, 1976, p. 32). As such, they seem to have operated in a way that did not push them to think about integrating the dimensions of a broader environment into their work.

The Limits of Political Structures and Processes

In those early days it was rare to find explicit attention to the impact of the structure and the political process within the US. While that structure and process produced policies that when adopted often required substantive trade-offs at the implementation stage, there was a tendency to avoid thinking seriously about implementation requirements during adoption. New programs rarely emerged from the policy adoption stage of the policy process with the clarity that was more likely to emerge from a parliamentary system. Major new programs and policies in the US were likely to contain conflicting elements that reflected the trade-offs that were made during adoption. If an adopted policy involved a set of new relationships, the legislative branch was likely to have to revisit the policy and clarify those relationships before the policy could be implemented. These trade-offs often produced conflicting values and approaches within the policy design that emerged from the extended political policy adoption process.

The importance of these trade-offs became more visible soon after the spread of the policy analysis function from DoD to other parts of the federal government in the US. The assumptions that were made by the earlier generation began to be challenged. Fewer agencies had environments that operated through predictable hierarchical relationships. Policy environments ranged from stable relationships to highly turbulent settings in which advocates of different approaches could be expected to emerge in policy discussions. While some environments had strong and unified players, others contained organizations with conflicting views that supported their belief that they all had a legitimate claim on aspects of many issues. Some of the players continued to be found within the government itself but increasingly policy systems included non-government players (both for-profit and non-profit organizations) concerned about the relevant policy.

As both analysts and clients began to focus on issues and programs that moved beyond the formulation stage of the policy process to include adoption, implementation and evaluation stages, they became more aware of the constraints that were established for them by the structure of the US political system. The US constitutional structure defined the environment in two important ways. First, the shared powers of the US three branches of government mean that many issues require some involvement of Congress, the court system and the executive branch. The structure of the US system actually encourages the three branches to approach policy issues in different ways. It is likely that structure provides the possibility (and often probability) that policy differences will emerge from that complex setting and that policy designs will likely be limited to <u>incremental directions</u> toward desired goals.

Second, the structure of US federalism (and other federal systems) creates tension between the national government and the states or provinces and often localities. Yet it was difficult to generalize about states since they differed so much from one another in terms of population characteristics, political structure and economic conditions. As globalism has increased over the years, it has also been obvious that countries with unitary systems have different responses to policy issues than those with shared power systems. When policy debates cross national and regional lines this structure is likely to lead to different policy approaches that often generate policy conflict. Unitary systems (such as parliamentary systems) seemed to be more conducive to the kind of policy analysis that had been put into place in the US in the 1960s and early 1970s than shared power systems.

A third area that produced complexity emerged as budget decisions made by the appropriations committees and subcommittees in Congress began to make substantive policies through the appropriations process. This set of decisions sometimes replaced the substantive policy approach that emerged from the perspective of the authorizing committees and subcommittees. The different perspectives of the two sets of committees and subcommittees (authorizing and appropriations bodies) created another set of conflicts.

Finally, another contributing factor to a turbulent environment is the timing and frequency of elections in a democracy. The US system of financing election costs often means that elected officials are always raising money for their next election the minute they are elected. Thus it is difficult for individuals elected to the US Senate for a six-year term to focus on their work developing new policies without thinking about where contributions will come from for their next election. Campaign finance reform efforts have not led to decreases in this form of political reasoning.

Changes in Decision-Making Processes

During the twenty-first century the policy environment has experienced new forms of decision-making that have changed expectations about the way that decisions are made. A concern about policies and programs that have some shared attributes but operate in separate decision-making processes has led to increased use of networks in decision-making. These networks reach across a range of organizational boundaries and often involve players concerned about the same issues but in significantly different ways. Like matrix organizations, these networks provide a setting for individuals and groups to negotiate recommendations that have a way of satisfying different players as they trade-off perspectives that might have created future problems.

[handwritten margin notes: networks / in theory / help / find / balance / to eliminate]

The diverse players in a network provide a way for analysts to think about multiple and often conflicting perspectives. Over the past several decades, it is clear that policy issues that had been defined as totally domestic concerns seem to involve global players. Yet this has been a difficult reach for many policy analysts and it has made an already complex policy environment even more difficult to conceptualize. As policy analysis as a field spread across the globe, the differences between activities found in the US and those in other countries began to emerge. In addition, policy norms were increasingly established by multinational organizations such as the European Commission and it is often difficult for analysts to figure out a way to deal with them. Multiple voices and interests are likely to emerge in reaction to different approaches whenever analysts attempt to look beyond their immediate settings.

[handwritten margin notes: future / risks? / to diff. / groups]

Developing a Conceptual Map

While policy analysts are usually familiar with the general concept of stakeholder analysis, they often rely on knowledge of highly visible and well-known officials and organizations when they use that technique (stakeholder analysis is a process that assesses changes to a system from the perspective of interested parties, called stakeholders). As policy environments have become more complex and involve actors and processes that may not be highly visible, some analysts have formalized a process that pushes them to create a map at the beginning of their analysis that produces a picture or check list that structures their work.

Maps can be relatively informal or more formal. Dobel and Day suggest that "many thoughtful maps originate on the back of an envelope or on a napkin in a coffee shop" (Dobel and Day, 2005, p. 2). But they do allow an analyst to identify pressures their organization face created by external forces such as elections, the economy, funding cuts or social movements and other organizations both inside government and outside of it. A map has the ability to help an analyst identify information sources that may not be traditional. It also provides a way to think about the staff within the client's organization (their training and expectations) as well as the values that are built into the day-to-day culture of the organization. The basic structure of the map provides a way for an analyst to look at formal actors in categories such as policymakers (including courts), resource controllers, internal staff and groups somewhat outside the governmental structure (constituents, interest groups, clients served and media). In addition, it can include outside forces such as economic and budget pressures, changing client needs, new technology, unemployment patterns and emerging competition.

Maps can also be used to group the nature of relationships between actors (where does the relationship exist and where should it move) and the quality of relationships (ranging from supportive to enemy relationships). It often produces odd bedfellows when analysts attempt to group participants as supporters, opponents or neutral to particular proposals or activities. It is not unusual for an analyst to discover that their client may emphasize a limited group of players who support some proposals but fail to consider reactions from other players who may have the ability to stop some paths of action. The analyst may generalize about a group of players but ignore conflicts within the group that emerge from generational or other differences. At the least, an attempt to broaden the analytic cast of characters through a map that includes multiple venues for action can be a way of anticipating opposition.

Dobel and Day have described mapping as "a means to larger ends." They note that the process produces cognitively clear and usable guides to chart and navigate the shifting political environment. Further, they note that "it begins with an understanding that all organizational success depends upon working with multiple actors in changing external and internal environments" (Dobel and Day, 2005, p. 21).

While mapping is probably not the only way to analyze the actors and interests in a policy environment, it does provide a way for an analyst to move beyond their personal experience and contacts often associated with political actors to devise a more systematic way of examining these actors and their interests. At the same time, this approach is rarely utilized in many analytic systems which rely only on formal data sources. Mapping actually provides a way for both analysts and clients to anticipate the likely source of policy battles that might emerge in the future.

There are different ways of presenting the mapping information. Figure 4.1 presents a format that can be used as a tool to depict the key actors and their influences. Analysts can use that structure to identify the role of various policymakers with authority (the courts, legislators

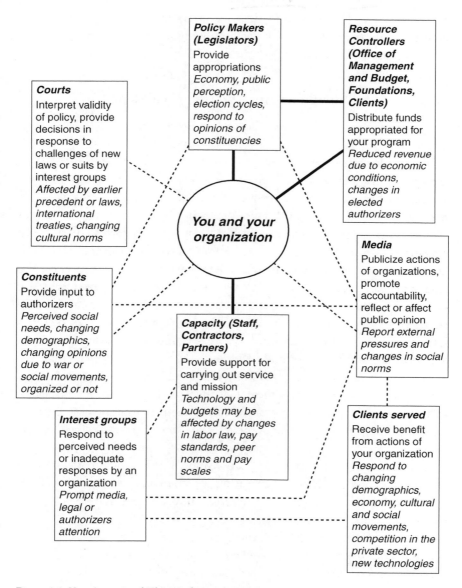

Figure 4.1 Key Actors and Their Influence.

Source: Dobel and Day, A Note on Mapping, 2005.

and resource controllers). The structure focuses on those within the organization who actually carry out the services and mission of the organization (a differentiation between career and political staff is often important). It also asks the analyst to think about the views of constituents, interest groups and clients served. This is particularly relevant in a situation where the environment is experiencing some form of change. Finally, analysts can include the role of media as they promote accountability relationships and public opinions about the issue.

When or Why Should an Analyst Produce a Map?

There are two possible traps involved in producing a map. The first – and most common – involves developing a map that is too narrow. Such a map would limit both the designation of potential players in the issue and the forces and structures that might play a role involving the issue. The second trap is one that produces such an extensive set of actors and issues that it is too broad and limits the utility of the map production.

Both of these traps can be avoided if the analyst thinks of this analytic exercise as a way of beginning the process by erring on the side of including players and issues. It is useful to begin the analysis by erring on the side of inclusion; that is, by thinking about possibilities that might not have been usual ways of thinking about the issue. The map can be used by the analyst himself or herself as a way of approaching the relevant issue in directions that may not have always come to mind. The analyst may or may not share the final map with the client. But producing such a map is a useful way of expanding traditional ways of looking at the issue and identifying more unusual or creative pathways for options. It may be possible for the analyst to turn the map into several possible scenarios that might be helpful to clients and others involved in the issue.

The cases that are used in this book illustrate a number of situations that seem to be useful in determining whether an actor or issue is relevant to include in a mapping effort. They provide examples of the following:

- The presence of future elections
- Dealing with uncertainty
- The balance between narrow and broad approaches
- The impact of federalism and/or centralized vs. decentralized systems

- Moving outside of the relevant bureaucracy/agency to
  - Other agencies
  - The legislative branch
  - Courts
- Including clients
- Issue tied to other issues
- Perspectives of staff within the agency
- Role of interest groups

Examples from the Cases

The Presence of Future Elections

James Williams was particularly sensitive to the past experience of the UK Labour Party when they developed an analytical process to determine the research budget for colleges and universities. That approach was believed to have contributed to Labour's loss at the time since it engendered criticism from traditional Labour supporters. Labour is currently leading a coalition government but is fearful of a loss in the future if the approach used in the past were to be adopted. Including the dynamics of an election environment in this case is both relevant and important.

Dealing with Uncertainty

Lisa Li has been given the assignment of developing a five-year strategic plan for the Hong Kong Education Bureau. She originally thought that the task was straightforward but realized that it is located within an environment of uncertainty. Part of the uncertainty relates to population changes in Hong Kong. But the major contribution to the uncertainty emerges from the changing political relationship between Hong Kong and the mainland. She believes that five-year strategic plans are probably more effective in predictable settings and doesn't know how to deal with the current situation. But she needs to be explicit about the presence of this environmental issue.

The Balance between Narrow and Broad Approaches

William O'Neill is a consultant who has been hired by a group of individuals to deal with a current problem involving Members of Parliament who were removed from their position because they had dual citizenship in both Australia and another country.

As he immersed himself in the issue he realized that it could be approached in very different ways. It could be defined as a legal issue, involving a section of the Australian Constitution. It could also be defined as a partisan political problem since the removal of some of the parliamentarians destroyed an existing political coalition. Or it could be defined as a long-standing immigration issue that related to the country's requirements and definition of citizenship and access to Australia. All three were possible but he wasn't sure how to determine the focus of the proposed map. He actually might use the three approaches as the basis for developing options and creating criteria that allow him to compare their strengths and weaknesses.

Veronica Lopez is confronted with a policy issue that encompasses two very different groups of players both inside and outside of the World Health Organization. She is very aware of the tension between the efforts of international health workers (who operate through formal national structures) and the global health networks (whose activities involve a range of non-state organizations and approaches). She was brought to World Health Organization (WHO) because of her knowledge about both types of efforts and the conflict that seemed to be increasing between them. She felt that the two efforts were leading to a gulf between those who had expertise in major health problems and those who had formal authority to deal with those issues.

As she tried to map the players involved in the issue she realized that both of the groups probably contained actors with diverse perspectives. Thus she couldn't assume that either of them would be able to agree on a single alternative and so her assignment required her to find ways to build coalitions both within and between them.

The Impact of Federalism and/or Centralized vs. Decentralized Systems

There is often a tendency for policy analysts to limit the players in a policy environment to the level of the organization structure where a client is found. Yet we know that many political structures are created in a way that involves other players at other levels. A policy could involve states or provinces or regional bodies even if they are not obviously visible in the traditional political structure. Several of the cases used in this analysis actually illustrate such a tendency.

James Marlin has been thinking about the next stages of federal activity involving rural policy in terms that illustrate his knowledge of the need to involve many state level actors in that activity. The earlier federal activity *emphasized the creation of state rural development councils who would work closely with their federal counterparts. But it is not clear how those councils would be involved in future efforts. In this case, he not only has to be sensitive to the federal-state relationship but also needs to acknowledge the differences between states as they approach the rural issues.*

Patrick Nonet has agreed to move from his job with the provincial government of Quebec to the Canadian national government. His knowledge of the bilingual language policy began with the Quebec experience 50 years ago and moved to the national level. That policy became an important factor in the effort to avoid Quebec succession. He is concerned that his new responsibility might require him to dramatically depart from his commitment to Quebec. He wants to keep his concern about that province alive but also recognize that there are other forces that work against that. Including a Quebec perspective in his map will help him manage that conflict.

Joyce Winter has a somewhat similar problem in terms of the relationship between the environmental perspective of California and that of the federal government. Her past experience did seem to give her a way of dealing with the structural conflict between the state and the federal government. The current conflict that emerged from the Trump administration seemed to require a different strategy than the one she had used in the past. She doesn't want to adopt an approach that leads to further conflict and so thinks that it may be time to put the issue on the agenda in a new way.

Colleen Hendricks is frustrated by the limited resources that are available to the City of New York to deal with the need for low-income housing. Over the years she has observed that the State of New York has significant resources available to cities and towns in the state to provide low-income housing. Her initial exploration of this resource base seems to suggest that it might be something that can be useful to the city. However, she does not know much about the decision process at the state level that seemed to limit NYC's ability to draw on the funds. She thinks it would be useful for her to explore that process as she develops the decision map for her issue.

WANG Liping found himself dealing with a policy environment that seemed to encompass much of the policy and political world. He knew it would be difficult to highlight one level of government action without creating distortions in another. Working at the international level had been somewhat easier because it involved conversations that were often abstract and general. But the closer he came to actions demanded from provinces or even countries, the more visible their effects became.

Moving Outside of the Relevant Bureaucracy/Organization to Other Agencies, the Legislative Branch and Courts

The political structure that organizes the authority framework around an issue provides a way of identifying players. The shared power system in the US provides a useful point of departure. However, there is a tendency for clients inside of government agencies to minimize the complexity of the other players involved.

For example, when people inside an agency often think about the legislative branch as "Congress" they are suggesting that the body operates as an entity. Such an approach ignores the two separate houses of Congress and the separation between authorizing and appropriations committees and subcommittees. All of these actors may have the potential of getting involved in the issue and producing diverse options. Similarly, the complexity of the twenty-first century world may mean that specific programs are located in cabinet departments that don't seem to be related to the program at hand either totally or through specific elements within the policy.

Marjorie Benson had expected to return to the Department of Health and Human Services after her maternity leave to continue her advocacy of the Affordable Care Act. The change in administration seemed to make that a less than appealing possibility. She decided to use the mapping exercise as a way of nominating some other possibilities. Were there other places in the department where the political environment might be less politicized? That could include both other analytic offices as well as program offices. Were there places in the congressional offices where concern about health services for the poor or rural residents would be more attractive to her?

Jonathan Weston had assumed a political job in the US Department of Energy thinking that his experience as a lobbyist for the windmill industry could be directly applied to his position. He soon learned two things. First, he became aware of the differences between the public and private sector. And second, he learned that his portfolio required him to become aware of other program elements within Energy but also other federal agencies such as EPA and the State Department. Those agencies took positions on issues that affected the windmill program and Weston began to learn about the reasons why that happened.

James Mason's concern about North Carolina's congressional map led him to closely follow the detailed reasoning of an opinion issued by a panel of federal judges.

He realized that it was important to learn more about the legal decision process and the likelihood that other panels of judges may be ready to issue a

Warning against one-size-fits-all policy impacts

ruling on this issue. Thus he used the mapping process as a way of exploring what may become an extremely important development. *Analysts too broadly defining who will be experiencing the policy needs more nuance*

Be Attentive to the Characteristics of Clients in the Map

Some public sector (and many private sector) programs define their clients in a very generic fashion and thus are not attentive to different groups within the general category of "clients." This tendency makes it difficult to determine who is actually impacted by the relevant program. Several of the cases used in this book have had to deal with that issue.

Renee Hernandez was hired by a consulting firm to develop a performance assessment of schools in Dallas, Texas. The school system served a very diverse group population but the information that was used in the assessment did not disaggregate by race or ethnicity. As such it did not have the ability to show how well the programs put in place were serving different population groups. Specifying the diversity during the mapping phase might have made that problem more obvious.

Curtis Brown's policy analysis might have been more useful if he had acknowledged the dimensions of the policy problem of overcrowding in terms of different categories of prisoners. That would have included attention to the severity of their crimes, their family location (urban or rural), the location of their crimes, and their race and ethnicity.

James Williamson's effort to define expectations about the needs and potential use of funds for higher education by various states seemed to be impacted by demands for a single model of use. His personal experience, however, indicated that it would be useful to acknowledge that a one-size-fits-all approach would not be effective. He might be able to characterize different approaches that might serve as an alternative method to that pressure if he made that diversity explicit in the mapping effort.

A similar approach might be used by Margaret Trumball as she sought to develop a migration policy for the European Commission of the EU. Instead of searching for a single policy, she could analyze the different ways in which member countries were approaching the policy problem. She might replace a single policy with different policy approaches that were based on different situations and expectations of the member countries. Specifying those differences in the map would support such a strategy and acknowledge the reality of those differences.

Issue Tied to Other Seemingly Separate Issues

Traditional approaches to policy analysis tend to seek clarity about the dimensions of a policy problem. Yet many issues operate in environments where multiple policies and programs interact with one another. *The efforts that predated James Marlin's rural development work indicated that there is more than one way to define "rural" and the problems in rural America cross many different policy sectors and programs. All of these efforts are justified because often they all have an impact on the same citizen or group. This clearly was something that Jonathan Weston learned when he realized that windmills operate in a complex environment.*

George Smith had a somewhat different realization when he saw that policies related to coal mining were linked to problems in the education sector. He found it difficult to think of a way to deal with that but it was useful for him to raise that in the mapping effort.

Marianne Williams's frustration seemed to be focused on the inability of the Baltimore Police Department and its mayor and city council to fail to see that criminal justice problems were directly linked to poverty, ineffective educational systems, limited housing and inadequate health programs. Again, the complexity of this issue could be signaled in the mapping effort and might actually have an impact on the client.

Perspectives of Staff within the Agency

Many policy settings are staffed by an array of people who represent different ways of looking at a set of policies and programs. These differences are based on diverse professional identities, educational background, socio-economic background and their roles within the organization. These differences are illustrated by several of the cases.

James Williams in the Prime Minister's Office in Great Britain is charged with developing the research budget for colleges and universities. His colleagues within the organization are likely to be other budget experts as well as individuals who are knowledgeable about educational policy in colleges and universities. It appears that the previous effort to focus on this budget area was not sensitive to the higher education culture and faced significant conflict between the two perspectives.

Patrick Nonet's move to the Canadian national government puts him in a setting which is likely to define the bilingual policy problem as a budget issue and to minimize its sensitivity to the symbolism of bilingualism. He will be surrounded by staff who are not likely to understand the meaning that he gives to that set of requirements.

Margaret Trumball is now operating in a staff setting that represents several disparate approaches to the migration issue. The expansion of the EU opened the door to staff drawn from a number of former Soviet Union countries. They had been socialized to work in a very different setting and they also had different experiences with the migration issue. Her experience and that of staff from the original EU countries tended to draw on practices borrowed from both France and the UK.

When Jonathan Weston joined the staff of the Department of Energy he realized that the existing career staff included a significant number of scientists. He found that the scientific culture was not only quite different from the private sector where he had spent much of his previous career but it was also different from the traditional training of a federal bureaucrat.

Role of Interest Groups

While interest groups are likely to appear in many mapping exercises, the developers of the maps do not always acknowledge the differences between types of interest groups (Wilson, 1989, pp. 79–83). Many students of bureaucracy tend to lump these four types together as generic interest groups.

It is quite common for policy issues to have interest groups that represent very different approaches and expectations. Thus it is important to acknowledge those differences in a mapping exercise since the conflict between groups can often be anticipated. James Q. Wilson defined four types of relationships between outside groups and agencies: Client agencies, entrepreneurial agency, interest group agencies and majoritarian agencies (Wilson, 1989, pp. 79–83). *For example, James Marlin can expect there to be disagreement between traditional agricultural interest groups and those that represent concerns that involve more generic "rural" issues. Similarly, Joyce Winter is likely to know that at least two different clusters of interest groups are likely to emerge when environmental issues are discussed – those who are regulated and those who seek regulation. And James Williams is likely to experience conflict between interest groups involving higher education that represent different types of institutions and geographic differences between them.*

Conclusions

This chapter has attempted to provide a reader with some suggestions for beginning a mapping exercise by erring on the side of inclusion of actors and issues. *When one reads the Reema Chatterjee case, it appears that she did not explore some of the problems that she and her family were likely to face when returning to India. What could she have included in her map that would have raised some of the issues that they experienced? India had changed and after 25 years in the US her family had different expectations about their lives.*

Maps are not magic answers to complicated problems but they do provide some information that can help an analyst prepare for the conflict and complexity that is likely to emerge.

5 The Policy Issue Itself

While we know that organizations, communities and political institutions have their own cultures, it is fairly rare that we look for cultures within policy areas. When we examine a specific policy across countries or within different population groups, we begin to see attributes that seem to be embedded in the activities associated with that particular policy sector. Yet few of us search for those attributes that do seem to be socially transmitted whenever a group of people engage in policy work in specific areas. It is actually rare for students of the policy field to focus on the diverse and often unique elements of different policies.

We are more likely to discover it when we focus on those who actually provide the service. Many policy fields seem to deal with it when they define the professional discretion that is present in a sector. For example, health policy exhibits conflict between the judgments of those who provide health services (who are often very protective of their autonomy and discretion) and those who pay for those services when they are translated into policies. Similarly, there is often a tension between the views of scientists involved in environmental policy and those who are concerned about the conflict between public goods and private rights.

This is not to say that these issues are always ignored. Specialization in a distinct policy area is a way to indirectly focus on those unique attributes. There are also other surrogates for culture. James Q. Wilson provided a framework that differentiated between types of agencies. He divided his analysis by asking two questions: Can the activities of their staff be observed? And can the results of those activities be observed?

The first question was answered by what he called "outputs" and the second "outcomes" (Wilson, 1989, p. 158). As he illustrated his typology, he found that it was very difficult to measure the outcome of the work of professionals since the profession itself controlled the expectations and norms of their work. While it might be described (through outputs), it is hard to measure its outcomes because the outcomes often rely on qualitative rather than quantitative aspects and often cannot be examined in a short-term perspective. In addition, Wilson's discussion of the differences in the political environments of agencies indicated different ways in which a policy sector relates to its external environment (Wilson, 1989, p. 79).

Wilson's typology does require policy analysts to be sensitive to the attributes of the sector in which they are working. It suggests that a one-size-fits-all approach is not likely to fit the issues and expectations found in very different settings. The mapping process often illustrates these differences (see Chapter 4) as an analyst attempts to comprehend the predictable dynamics associated with the policy problem.

In addition, a democratic society as large and diverse as the US is likely to produce very few policy issues in which there is agreement on the next steps to take to deal with a national policy problem. Other democratic systems face very similar situations. Given that, it is rare that policy issues find clear pathways or are responsive to technical "fixes." As such, the information that is available to an analyst through the mapping exercise is often evidence of the complexity of the cast of characters who are concerned about the policy issue.

How did the Problem Emerge?

Analysts often find that the problem they are encountering is not new. It may have new attributes at a particular time but it often relates to pressures and problems that emerged in a different form at an earlier time. The specific problem may have emerged because of a crisis or was tied to external events that opened up a new set of issues. Or, as John Kingdon suggested, (Kingdon, 1984) it surfaced because of "windows opening."

When the analyst is familiar with the policy sector, he or she may recognize that the problem that was assigned to the analyst is similar to issues faced in the past. Sometimes the problem is actually the same but cloaked in a new wrapping. But, conversely, the problem may actually be different because of changes in the external environment. For example, players in the past may have changed their positions. They may be responding to shifts in the political environment (such as elections). And those shifts can sometimes be quite dramatic. It is often useful to have a combination of veteran and novice players involved in the analytical process to bring both the past and the present to the endeavor. Some policy analysis scholars have also suggested that policy issues have a life cycle and are likely to respond differently when they are "mature" rather than "adolescents."

Examples from the Cases Dealing with the Way That the Policy Issue Emerges

Three of the cases illustrate different ways that a policy issue has emerged and landed on the analyst's desk. Marjorie Benson was on maternity leave when there was a change in the White House. As a result, when she returned to the office she found dramatic changes facing her. Her past commitment to the health policy area does not seem to fit the new surroundings. She is trying to figure out whether she can find a way to exist in that environment and contribute to what she sees as an effective health policy.

James Mason has been involved in the legal challenge to North Carolina's congressional map mostly as a citizen. The recent decision by a panel of federal judges struck down that map, condemning it as unconstitutional because it was drawn to support the Republicans' political advantage. A new Democratic governor has been recently elected at the same time that Trump was elected president and Mason thinks there may be an opportunity for him to find a job taking advantage of those changes.

Lisa Li is a new Administrative Officer in the Hong Kong Education Bureau and has been tasked with an assignment that involves the development of a five-year strategic plan for the bureau. She has learned that this assignment is not a technical challenge but is actually a major political test of her ability to deal with the uncertainty that has emerged from the changing political relationship between Hong Kong and the mainland. She is also facing changes in the student population in the schools in Hong Kong. The private international schools in the city are now largely populated with mainland Chinese students.

WANG Liping has found himself dealing with the substance of the environmental issue that has moved far beyond his earlier work on its international dimensions. His work on the Paris Agreement did not push him to focus on issues that responded to unique domestic impacts that varied in terms of the experience of different provinces and industries. He found himself learning about both the political and economic perspectives in these settings. Yet it was not always clear to him how these variations could be aggregated, if at all.

At What Stage of the Policy Process is the Problem Located?

For many years the policy literature has noted that policy activities follow patterns that are identifiable as discrete systems and processes. While different writers have depicted the stages somewhat differently, they generally follow five stages over time: Agenda setting, formulation, adoption, implementation and evaluation. Each of the stages has its own functional demands and its own institutional setting but operates within an overall process that is continuous and open-ended. As a policy issue moves over time new opportunities and constraints are attached to the issue as different actors are involved. The result is a situation in which issues are reopened that appear to have been settled at an earlier point in the decision-making process. And new answers may emerge from those shifts. Thus an analyst is likely to find that the problem at hand both reopens old issues and also asks different questions because the policy issue has moved into another stage of the process.

It is important to be clear about the stage of the process that confronts the analyst. It is not unusual for an analyst to be faced with a policy problem that takes place in the stage of a policy but the problem itself was created by earlier decisions within the process. Brewer and deLeon (1984.) suggested that the movement of an issue from one setting to another provides the opportunity for shifts in both process as well as substance. While the process may be depicted as a closed process, in reality there are shifts that occur both within and between the stages.

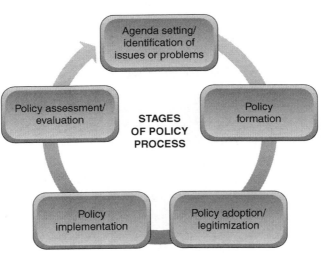

Figure 5.1 Stages of Policy Process.

Ensure you're aware of what stage you're in.

This has created a fragmented, pluralistic system of policy making that is pulled along by the relatively predictable behavior of multiple actors who must deal with the imperatives of political demands, time and deadlines. While it is not machine-like, it does contain elements of predictability at the same time it is constantly modified (Radin, 2013, p. 219).

Examples from the Cases That Relate to the Stages of the Policy Process

Two of the cases illustrate challenges to experienced analysts who want to find a way to get their policy concerns on the policy agenda. *Joyce Winter is a well-known policy analyst who has dealt with environmental issues in California for years. She has been very concerned about the conflict between California policies and those of the federal government. She knew that the current situation called for an atypical policy analysis approach that helped to put the issue on the agenda. But she wasn't sure about the form that would take. Should she create a new organization, commission a study or book, or identify leaders in such an effort?*

William O'Neill is a consultant in Canberra, Australia who has been contacted by several individuals who are concerned about the removal of several elected members from Parliament because they (some actually unknowingly) had dual citizenship in both Australia and another country. Like Joyce Winter, he is also looking for a way to put the issue on the agenda to make sure that it won't happen again.

Who are Supporters and Opponents of Probable Options?

The constant changes created by different stages of the policy process also mean that there can be different coalitions of both supporters and opponents as the issue moves over time. Some issues, however, are more stable and predictable than others. But political shifts can upend coalitions and thus it is important to revisit the probable involvement of actors both inside the decision-making system and outside of it.

The fluidity of the situation may require a re-examination of both the perceived causes of the policy problem as well as the options that may be devised to address the problem. An analyst should not be surprised that the definition of the causes of the policy problem can both change and become more complex over time. Probably the definition may also become clearer over time but that is not usual.

Can make dif maps for each stage of the process.

Policy issue gone wrong?
REFRAME!

This can occur because past efforts to deal with the issue are often crafted in incremental terms. The partial movement may actually further complicate the issue. Past analysts and decisionmakers may have determined that a partial solution was better than nothing at all. Criticism of past definitions of policy problems can lead to attempts to reframe the policy issue altogether. Sometimes this reframing can even change the definition of the issue by moving it from one policy sector to another.

Opiate issue reframed

from blaming addicts to blaming drug companies — also reframing in terms of race

Examples from the Cases that Emerge from Changes in the Environment

James Williams has been assigned to a new policy analysis unit in the Prime Minister's Office in Great Britain. His specific assignment was to come up with a research budget for colleges and universities that could be defended in Parliament and which was based on a rational analysis. He realizes that his assignment is a replay of one that was given to his predecessor the last time Labour was in power. That policy opened up conflict between two strong education interest groups and, as a result, the implementation of the policy turned out to be highly problematic. He is not sure whether similar action would create the kind of conflict that did lead to Labour's loss of control the last time.

Why is an Analysis Thought to be Useful?

It is not always clear why a client believes that a policy analysis is appropriate and useful. In some settings commissioning an analysis is institutionalized in the standard operating procedures of an organization. As such, the analysis takes its place paralleling previous work and can be viewed as a step in an approach that can provide a form of monitoring for the client. In other cases the analysis is commissioned because a new problem has emerged and the client wants some new perspectives on the policy issue. In still other cases, the analysis becomes an assessment of earlier decisions and is expected to provide a new decision pathway.

The timing of the commissioning of an analysis may coincide with the entrance of new decisionmakers in the organization who may or may not agree with the approaches taken by their predecessors. At one point in the 1970s congressional committees in the US actually commissioned evaluations that were timed to be completed when the authorizing committees faced deadlines for reauthorization of specific programs.[1]

timing matters

The diversity of methodologies and approaches found in policy analysis activities across the globe has provided the field with a range of choices that span both narrow and broad approaches. The analysis could be a "quick and dirty" analysis that draws on earlier work in the policy sector. Or it could be a multi-year effort that is based on the collection of new data. The longer-term analyses often have lost their original clients because of constant changes in political leadership in an organization. As such the completion of the analysis may not coincide with the policy needs of a particular time and cast of characters.

When policy analysts operate from permanent organizational settings, there is often an institutional memory contained in the relevant staff. Those analysts bring both strengths and weaknesses. They are often very familiar with the policy area and provide an institutional memory about the policy sector to the client. But if they have been in the organization for many years they are sometimes known for their particular policy approach and thus their work is predictable. The fairly widespread use of consultants in policy analysis also has its own set of strengths and weaknesses. Consultants often do not have past experience in the policy sector but they may bring in new approaches to the issue that is useful. Since many of the consultants have both private sector and public sector clients, they may not be familiar with the differences between the two sectors.

Examples from the Cases That Illustrate Assumptions about the Utility of an Analysis

Patrick Nonet recently moved from a job with the provincial government of Quebec to the Canadian national government. He was known as a strong advocate for the bilingual language approach over the years. He is reaching retirement age and was brought to Ottawa to head up the staff of a Prime Minister's commission that will examine the future of the existing bilingual policy. Over the years since the original act was passed, there has been a decline in the proportion of Canadians who are using French as their native language. Given fiscal realities, there is a movement to change the policy. The commission is expected to issue a report that will examine both the economic rationale for a change of policy as well as the symbolism of the existing policy.

Renee Hernandez was hired by a consulting firm in Dallas, Texas to work on their contract with the Dallas School District that calls for a performance measurement process assessing faculty performance and student results to measure effectiveness. Such a system is now in place and she is expected to work on it. As a Hispanic young woman, she is particularly sensitive to the diversity in the student body. She sees that past efforts were largely focused on the needs of African American students and faculty and has observed that there was more attention to their problems than to those of Hispanics in the system. Her personal values were difficult to apply to the existing system, especially decisions about closing schools that would impose difficulties for Hispanic students. She thought that her views were likely to collide with those that were found in the consulting firm's contract.

Should the Analyst Always Make a Recommendation to the Client, Choosing between Policy Options/Alternatives?

The classic work on the policy analysis process, Bardach and Patashnik's *A Practical Guide for Policy Analysis* (2016), suggests that policy analysis moves through eight stages that conclude with a recommendation to a client. This advice made a lot of sense in the early stages of the policy analysis field when it was assumed that a client had direct involvement with a single client and the conflict that might have been a part of the analysis could be handled in analytical terms.

While that continues to be good advice in many situations, the changes that have taken in the policy analysis process have produced areas of conflict that cannot be dealt with analytically. This is particularly present in situations of high levels of conflict that emerge from the need to satisfy very diverse actors who are a part of the client role. For example, analysts in the Congressional Research Service (CRS) in the US Library of Congress often produce work that offers their clients a range of options but does not make a choice between them.

Stopping the analysis with specification of options and not a recommendation is justified on several grounds. First, the client for CRS work is usually the congressional committee or subcommittee with authority in the policy area. That body is composed of representatives from both political parties who often have very different approaches to the policy issue. Second, policy analysis is often very effective in clarifying the issues for the clients. Carol Weiss called this role "enlightenment" and argued that it is often an important way of assisting decisionmakers. Her work contrasts the multiple roles played by analysis in the legislative branch (Weiss, 1989). While her analysis focuses on the legislative uses, her typology is also relevant to other settings.

Examples from the Cases That Do Not Include a Recommendation

Margaret Trumball recently moved from the United Nations headquarters in New York to the European Commission headquarters in Brussels. She was assigned to the migration policy unit in the commission whose top official was from Poland. While she knew something about the migration issue, her experience at the UN was quite different than that at the European Commission. She realized that the migration issue was immediate and problematic for some of the member nations while others were not as concerned about it. The differences were especially clear after the expansion of EU membership following the collapse of the Soviet Union. After immersing herself in the issue, she thought that the situation suggested that her product as a policy analyst would not make a single recommendation but, rather, would provide alternatives to be considered by the individual countries. She hoped that her analysis would provide a framework that would allow the members to discuss the issue and craft a decision that was agreeable to them.

James Williamson had been recently hired by a consortium of foundations that supported higher education programs for students from families who did not have the resources to pay for college for their children. While new to this job, he was quite familiar with its activities. His current task was to define expectations about the use of the consortium's funding. Over the past 15 years he had been employed by two of the state agencies that received funds from the consortium. His past experience made him sensitive to differences in the structure of the state government, the demographic composition of the population in the state and the financial conditions that set the context for allocation of expenditures. In addition, he was not as familiar with the expectations of the members of the program's board. Given all of this, he was wary of jumping into a highly structured set of requirements. He thought of two alternative strategies. One would be to only develop options, not a recommendation. The other strategy would involve an incremental approach, focusing on one set of issues at a time rather than a total package or viewing the options as different processes (rather than substantive policy suggestions).

WANG Liping thought he was taking a leap of faith when he identified the members of a group that would advise him. He drew the members from bodies that each had unique think tank capacities, responding to different theoretical perspectives as well as immediate policy problems. He doubted whether the six members had ever had contact with one another or even saw themselves occupying shared policy space.

Is it Important to Spend Time on the Way That the Policy Issue is Framed?

Since policy issues don't remain static it is not surprising that a policy issue could actually be defined in multiple ways. These diverse definitions place the problem in quite different contexts; some of them contribute to the conflict and complexity faced by policy analysts. Three examples from the recent past illustrate this dilemma. Framing turns out to be a very important and difficult set of decisions for policy analysts.

First, efforts to create rural development programs have traditionally been located in the US Department of Agriculture despite the reality that many rural citizens are not involved in farming and their lives involve problems that have moved far away from agricultural experiences. Even the definitions of "rural" used by various parts of the federal government suggest that there is not clarity about the appropriate category for these issues.

The second example involved a policy that would allow the provision of new needles for drug users in exchange for existing needles. This was based on research within the public health agencies in the Department of Health and Human Services that showed that programs for the exchange of used needles for new needles were able to reduce the incidence of HIV in that population. The Secretary of HHS was about to make an announcement about this program when the staff of the White House Office of National Drug Control Policy argued that providing needles for drug users would encourage drug use. HHS's decision was based on a public health frame while those in the White House saw the problem as a criminal justice issue.

The third example of issues related to framing was built into the US Federal Community Development Block Grant program. Localities and states were given the opportunity to choose how to frame their application around multiple policy areas. These could or could not include housing, economic development, employment or environment. Yet when some policy analysts were charged with an evaluation of the program they decided that the program should be more narrowly focused on economic development.

It seems that questions and concerns about the framing process can surface both at the beginning of a policy analysis effort as well as midway through the activity.

Framing Examples from the Cases

William O'Neill from Canberra, Australia is faced with a policy issue that is extremely difficult to define and frame. He immersed himself in the details of the policy against Members of Parliament holding dual citizenship in both Australia and another country. He realized that the policy could be framed in three different ways. First, it could be defined as a legal issue based on Section 44 of the Australian constitution. But he wasn't sure whether than captured the complexity of the issue. Second, he could frame it as a residue of Australia's colonial past with England. The early settlers after independence still had citizenship in the UK in the period termed "White Australia policy." Third, immigration patterns indicated that new residents were coming from non-European descent. The concept of multiculturalism became the norm. But by the twenty-first century citizenship increased residence requirements and introduced a citizenship test. In recent years, Australia seemed to be following a trend set by immigrant-receiving countries of Western Europe and was less inclusive. O'Neill realizes he has significant relevant ways to frame this issue.

James Marlin's experience with rural development policies had been organized through activities of a loosely defined network that included a wide range of players from multiple federal agencies, states, localities, non-profit groups and the private sector. It continued its program in a non-traditional way, avoiding traditional federal government formalism. His framing problem revolved around the choice of whether the activity could continue to exist in its non-formal ways or whether it needed to develop formal mechanisms that allowed it to operate with budget, authority and a formal structure.

He was particularly concerned about what would happen when an administration changed and participants were drawn to respond to formal accountability requirements.

Ellen Winston's interest in policy analysis revolved around its close relationship to research in welfare policy. She found herself in an organization that included both policy research activities and policy lobbying. When she joined the organization she thought that combination was likely to be very effective. However, as time went on, she saw that the two sets of activities were very difficult to combine, especially for someone committed to research norms. She was not sure whether her expectations were realistic. She thought that both research and lobbying were important but it was difficult to find ways to make the two processes more compatible. She wasn't sure she wanted to move along that pathway.

Jonathan Weston approached his position as a political appointee in the US Department of Energy assuming that his private sector expertise about windmill manufacturing would be easily transferred to the government activity involving windmills. His position did not require Senate confirmation and he felt that his past experience had prepared him for the job. He was known as someone who believed that the industry needed flexibility to be a viable manufacturer and his role in the government provided him with the opportunity to make sure that happened.

After six months he began to realize that his new role was quite different than he had assumed. The career staff members raised issues that were new to him. The alternatives that were developed in the memos they gave him included the perspective of players that he had never considered before but were involved in the decision-making process. He began to realize that the requirements that he had labeled "administrative burdens" imposed by the government on the private sector were intrinsic and appropriate for the public sector role. That really surprised him. He wasn't sure how to deal with this discovery.

Curtis Brown works for the Virginia Department of Corrections and has been handed an assignment that is puzzling to him. For the most part, the state's prison system has relied on prisons planned and run by the state government. The current secretary of the department has been pressured to find a way to utilize the private sector in the current effort to expand the prison system and meet the political demands of the state population.

Brown is comfortable dealing with this issue when it is framed as a public sector issue but doesn't know how to deal with it if it involves the private sector for either planning or operation of the system. He is trying to differentiate between the strengths and weaknesses of the two sectors but feels that the two worlds are quite different. He doesn't know whether it would be possible to combine the involvement of the two and whether such a combination will achieve either technical or political goals.

How Can a Policy Analyst Deal with Personal Values and Past Experiences that are Entwined with an Issue?

As some of the cases discussed in this book indicate, many people who become policy analysts come into this diverse profession with a personal commitment to specific issues and the policies developed to deal with a perceived problem. Those commitments often emerge when they have difficulty disentangling an analyst role from that of an advocate. They might search for a client who shares their values and thus find their role justified by the client's expectations. But that isn't always possible and the uncertainty built into the policy world may mean that a comfortable position at one point in time does not continue.

Thus it is challenging for a novice policy analyst to attempt to conceptualize a career pathway. This is challenging from the early stages of a career onwards. Often a new MPP takes a beginning job because of the nature of the competitive job market. Individuals who do have a personal commitment to a specific policy issue may find themselves in a position that is almost entirely technocratic and really far removed from the politics and issues embedded in the policy issue itself. Others may find ways to bring their personal values to the role. Often that is surprising and unexpected.

Examples from the Cases That Show Value Conflicts

Marianne Williams has worked for the Baltimore Police Department for three years and has found that she has significant problems with the performance measurement activities that have been undertaken by the department. The original activity was undertaken by the Mayor and city council who were focused on the performance of the department as a whole. Expectations were defined based on performance measures that would treat the various elements and activities of the department alike. The Performance-Stat process that was used did not really focus on differences between various parts of the city. The agenda for the effort was based on efficiency norms and an effort by the Mayor and city council to control the department. But the death of Freddie Gray – an African American who died in police custody – became a focusing event in the city and caused her to rethink the performance assessment process. She believed that the process should be revised and reframed to focus on differences across the city that might have resulted from diverse populations and very different settings.

Colleen Hendricks is a classic New Yorker whose personal values and interests led her to a job at the New York City Housing Authority. After five years at the job she grew restless because she saw that funds for low-income housing were available at the state level and didn't seem to move down to the city government. She did know that the allocation patterns for those funds were not always based on need but were allocated based on geographic criteria. That contributed to the problem that she identified. But she thought that it might be worth the effort to move to Albany and see whether she could have an impact on the process.

Reema Chatterjee felt that she should take advantage of the offer from the IMF in Washington to claim early retirement. Both she and her husband (who

*was at the World Bank) thought the offer provided them with an opportunity
to move back to India, spend time with their parents and open up a consulting
firm in Delhi that drew on their past career. While they had made regular visits
to India over the 25 years they lived in the US, they were not prepared for the
changes that had taken place in the political, social and economic environments. Their children were not happy about moving to India. Housing and
living prices were higher than expected. And it wasn't clear whether their
professional expertise would allow their consulting firm to thrive.*

Conclusions

The complexity of the policy analysis process often revolves around
issues and processes that involve the dimensions of the policy issue itself.
Some issues are intrinsically loaded with personal and value conflicts
that directly involve the client as well as the analyst. Others operate in a
policy environment that is unstable and populated by dramatically
different assumptions about the issue. Sometimes both policy analysts
and their clients tend to treat their analytical assignments as straightforward and do not take the time to define the assumptions and conflicts
that are contained in the assignment.

As noted earlier, democratic societies (particularly those that are large
and diverse) are not likely to produce policy issues in which there is
agreement on the next steps to take to deal with a national policy
problem. While those who approach a policy issue as a technical problem
may want to avoid that acknowledgment, it is useful for both clients and
analysts to acknowledge that it is rare that policy issues find clear pathways that do not require negotiation and compromise between the relevant players.

Note

1 Many of these evaluations were in the education policy area.

6   Information and Evidence

During the early stages of the policy analysis profession, faith in the methodologies of the analyst rested on a rarely articulated assumption that information was available and appropriate. Few analysts would have made this argument explicitly; they tended to rely on approaches that assumed information was out there, waiting to be plucked like low-hanging fruit on a tree. Not only was the information ready to be picked, but there was also an unarticulated belief that it would be easy to find "objective information" and that one could disentangle fact from value.

To some extent, it is unfair to describe this attitude as naïve. The views about information were not made explicit; rather, they were implicit in the conceptual paradigms that informed the early policy analysts. The twin frameworks of normative economics and positivist social science each had their own particular spins on this issue. For the economist, if one assumed that the market operated on the basis of perfect information, then it was not a great leap to assume that the marketplace of ideas also rested on such information. For the social scientist, reliance on the scientific method assumed that information could be objective, value free and available for all to use to further test hypotheses. Neither group questioned its ability to differentiate the true from the false and to provide advice to decisionmakers based on that confidence.

These approaches to the information task did not appear to be influenced by the experience of others whose perspectives were less technical. It is interesting that one of the earliest policy advisors, Kautilya, thought about information in a highly strategic fashion. In the fourth century BC, Kautilya devised an intelligence system in which spies who were trained and organized by the institute of espionage were posted throughout the realm in India (Goldhamer, 1978).

Max Weber considered information an instrument of power that should be treated as such. Weber argued that, as an important resource, information was to be guarded and held closely (Gerth and Mills, 1946, p. 233). He wrote:

> Every bureaucracy seeks to increase the superiority of the profession-ally informed by keeping their knowledge and intentions secret. Bureaucratic administration always tends to be an administration of "secret missions": in so far as it can, it hides its knowledge and action from criticism.... The concept of the "official secret" is the specific invention of bureaucracy, and nothing is so fanatically defended by the bureaucracy as this attitude.

This approach was quite different from the one that valued scientific open-ness and information sharing. Those assumptions were found in the work of some of the early policy analysts, particularly those who were rooted in the professional norms of the behavioral social sciences. Others did understand the differences between the experience of more traditional academics and those of individuals who focused on policy analysis as advisers but they did not seem to influence the early phase of practice. Both Aaron Wildavsky and Charles Lindblom acknowledged the limits of the academic approach. As Rein and White suggested, we should recognize that concern about an issue and action forces an analysis; it is not the other way around (Rein and White, 1977, p. 32). Vining and Weimer's differentiation between policy analysis and policy research (see Chapter 3) is an important conceptual framework that is useful in approaching the information topic.

Attitudes about information have become much more complex in the decades that have elapsed since the practice of policy analysis began. We have given attention to the definition of information, the kinds of information that are appropriate, sources of information, the need for it, as well as its functions and uses. We have become much more sophistic-ated about the limits of the original views that were embedded in the conceptual paradigms and analytic approaches used by the early analysts. Though it is not clear that we have agreed on an alternative approach that would replace the academically based social science framework, we are increasingly moving to an approach that emphasizes the interrela-tionship between information and social interaction and emphasizes the unique needs of policy analysis.

At the same time, policy analysts have increasingly defined their role around the use of complex quantitative analytic techniques. These tech-niques rely on the availability of data sources that are required to apply these methods. Advances in information technology have produced what is often called "big data" and contributed to efforts that mine the information found in social media. Analysts have often begun their work by framing it within the context of existing data systems. Often these systems were designed for specific purposes that can be quite different from the policy problem at hand. Such a condition may push the analyst away from the specific needs of a client or the unique demands of the policy problem at the core of the assignment.

Defining Information

The question "What is information?" would have seemed trivial when the policy analysis field was emerging. There were obvious answers to the question, depending on the framework that the analyst brought to the task at hand. When information is defined by an experimental mode with roots in the controlled laboratory setting, the imperatives of the scientific method make it clear what information is appropriate and what should be collected and analyzed. Similarly, those who operate from an economic paradigm, based on the imperatives of a market, would seek other kinds of information. Stone describes this information as of two varieties: "Objective" information about the price and quality of alternatives and "subjective" information about personal preferences (Stone, 1997).

Harold Wilensky suggested that the information relevant to policy – what he calls "intelligence" – includes questions, insights, hypotheses and evidence. He noted that it "includes both scientific knowledge and political or ideological information, scientific or not" (Wilensky, 1967, p. xiii). He defined a set of criteria that allow information to become intelligence: Clear, timely, reliable, valid, adequate and wide ranging. Charles Lindblom and David Cohen created a term to describe the approach to information that emerges from academic social science. They called it Professional Social Inquiry and contrasted it with what they called Usable Knowledge. This type of argument is similar to the differentiation that Vining and Weimer have made between policy research and policy analysis (Lindblom and Cohen, 1989, p. 8).

In her work on the use of information in Congress, Weiss differentiated between three categories of information: Policy information, political intelligence and analytic work. She argued that analytic information serves four main functions. First, it provides support for members' existing policy positions, allowing members to mobilize support from other

3 Types of Info + 4 Reasons for analytic info

members and strengthen their coalitions. Second, it serves as a warning system, signaling that something should be done. Third, it provides guidance that allows staff and members to design strategies and procedures or fine-tune existing procedures. Fourth, it offers a source of what Weiss calls "enlightenment," helping staff and members reconceptualize issues, modifying their thinking and offering new ways of thinking about issues.[1] Weiss has depicted the function of information as support for a pre-existing position, warning, guidance and enlightenment. She has described the uses to which it is put as political ammunition, reordering the agenda, design of activities and modification in thinking (Weiss, 1983).

What Kinds of Information Are Appropriate?

Bardach has noted that policy analysts need information for three principal purposes: First, to assess the nature and extent of the problem; second, to assess the particular features of the specific policy situation; and third to assess policies that have been thought by some to work effectively in similar situations (Bardach, 2009).

Because the early policy analysts were most likely to focus on the creation of new policies, the data they sought was frequently information that documented the need for the policy (conditions that caused the problem within the society or organization) and sometimes provided a general sense of how a proposed policy would operate. By the time that analysts were dealing with problems that emerged from existing policies (highlighting the implementation process) they were faced with complex relationships and issues that emerged from existing operations.

At that point, analysts looked to information that was already collected for assistance. In some instances, information that was collected to monitor agencies was the only information that was available but it did not always address the problems that these analysts were addressing. It was not unusual for organizations to collect information at an aggregate level that highlighted the formal accountability relationships in a hierarchical structure. It was not common in many settings to present data that was disaggregated by race, gender or other specific population categories. And it most often relied on data that was compatible with presentation in a quantitative form rather than qualitative definitions. The type of data sought was conditioned by the analytic techniques chosen by the analyst or the client.

What Are the Sources of Information?

Over the years policy analysts have drawn on many different sources of information. As noted earlier, the choice of tools or analytic method can predetermine the information source. At one point, Bardach suggested that the appropriate techniques for the policy analyst were more like those of a journalist than a social scientist. Others have described the data that is used by policy analysts as information that is "found" rather than manufactured. Martha Feldman described the process as one in which information is found in unexpected places or gathered in unconventional ways (Feldman, 1989, pp. 20–1). Others have relied on visits to organizations and agencies to observe the practices related to the policy problem. Some analysts have found ways of utilizing information produced by social media to illustrate different behaviors.

The practice in the twenty-first century of involving both private sector and public sector institutions in policymaking has led to difficulties when the private sector considers information to be of a proprietary nature. Similarly, a federalism structure can make it difficult to collect comparable information from local, provincial or state sources.

The Emergence of the Evidence Movement

Around 2010 a new approach to information emerged in the US and in a number of other countries. In many ways it was a variation on the academic approaches that had already been a part of the policy analysis field. Called the evidence movement it was a new way of searching for political neutrality. It was similar to the Planning, Programming System (PPBS) in the 1960s and reflected a belief in the potential of analytic skills and the ability to devise a rational framework that would produce neutral data. *Assumptions that info*

PPBS was followed by other efforts that rested on several assumptions: *is* That information is available, that information is neutral, that it is pos- *neutral* sible to define cause-effect relationships, and that almost all activities can be measured and quantified. Many analysts thought that this information could serve as the tool for defining the policy problem, as the way of choosing between options, and as the way of making a recommendation.

Giandomenico Majone was one of the more critical observers of these efforts. He viewed the analyst as one who plays the role of participant and mediator rather than objective scientist (Majone, 1989). Evidence for him was much closer to the process used in legal reasoning; it was information that was used to make a case.

But the faith in information was particularly important in the emergent evaluation field. Alice Rivlin described the federal government in the late 1960s. She commented that:

> Both advocates and evaluators were naïve by today's standards. We all thought that simple interventions could change lives and evaluation would show clear results quickly. It gradually dawned on all of us that progress was going to be more complicated.
>
> (Rivlin, 2015)

The use of the term "evidence" in this setting was very different from the way that "evidence" is defined in the legal system. In that system the advocate determines the best solution to a client's problem and the term "evidence" refers to anything that can be used to justify that solution. Evidence thus can be used to prove that something exists or proof that other perspectives are not true.

Despite the legal profession's claim to the concept of evidence, the US Congress enacted legislation in 2016 creating the Commission on Evidence-Based Policymaking. The commission was given a year "to study and develop a strategy for strengthening government's evidence building and policymaking efforts" (Report of the Commission on Evidence-Based Policymaking, 2017, p. 1). It highlighted its goal: "Rigorous evidence is created efficiently, as a routine part of government operations, and used to construct effective public policy." The commission argued that "the greater use of existing data is now possible in conjunction with stronger privacy and legal protections, as well as increased transparency and accountability."

According to the commission, this effort grew out of the historical view in the US recognizing the importance of the role of the Census Bureau in providing information for governance and, as well, the data provided in units within the government to develop policy information. The report defined "evidence" as information produced by "statistical activities" with a "statistical purpose" and envisioned a strong role for the centralized budget office (that would be the US Office of Management and Budget).

In addition to the role defined by the Report of the Commission on Evidence-Based Policymaking, the "evidence movement" has moved in several other directions. A group of social policy experts (called the Friends of Evidence) has attempted to focus on defining what constitutes useful and usable evidence, not that all information is appropriate. Others have linked the movement to a single research methodology – randomized controlled trials. Still others have argued that traditional social science (such as program evaluation) can be combined with data science (big data, data mining, predictive modeling and artificial intelligence).

The expectations surrounding the "evidence movement" do not always match the situations that policy analysts find themselves in. There is a range of constraints that have limited their application. The cases that are used in this book provide examples of problem areas that make the use of information more complex and difficult than the assumptions of those who advocate reliance on traditional statistical methods. These problem areas include:

- Multiple goals in many public policy problems and programs
- Can one learn from the past?
- Anticipating uncertainty and change
- Responding to cultural norms
- Dealing with an advocacy role
- The limits of formal data systems
- Limits of research produced data
- Ability of information to facilitate bargaining and trade-offs

Multiple Goals in Many Public Policy Problems and Programs

It is not surprising that the public sector in the twenty-first century faces many policy problems that do not lend themselves to a simple solution. This occurs because the issues involve multiple clients and decisionmakers who also operate in environments of uncertainty. It is particularly difficult to disentangle the ambiguity that may be found in the issue itself. It is common for analysts to be faced with multiple ways of defining the problem itself as well as multiple and often conflicting possible solutions. As such, these situations can overwhelm an analyst and make it difficult for that person to identify a single information source.

Margaret Trumball's assignment at the European Commission was to deal with the migration policy issue. She knew that each of the members of the EU had their own quite unique experience with the problem but they all had a voice in the decision-making process. She also knew that the staff at the commission brought their own personal views about the problem and, based on their country of origin, their preferred approach to it. She thought it might be possible to develop a typology that defined these different experiences. But given the differences, it was not likely to be based on comparable data sets. Rather, it was likely to be something like a comparative assessment of different case experiences from member countries. In addition, she observed that the issue itself was laden with conflicting values and it would be difficult to argue that there was only one way to deal with the issue.

James Marlin faced a somewhat similar problem as he tried to develop a strategy for continuing the US Department of Agriculture's efforts on rural issues. The past efforts involving this issue had generated a rich mixture of participants that represented multiple federal agencies as well as many state rural development councils. These state bodies included federal, state, local and tribal governments as well as non-profit and for-profit groups.

For nearly a decade Marlin had proceeded without formal public sector authority. His effort had no real budget or formal structure and, as a result, did not have to answer to traditional accountability requirements. States varied quite dramatically in their operation since they tried to deal with the unique realities in each of their settings. The experience suggested that each state and federal agency had their own unique story.

Like Trumball, the information that was likely to be useful to him was likely to be descriptive and qualitative. He did not think that a single model that could be used by all of the participants was appropriate.

Can One Learn from the Past?

James Williams found himself in a new policy unit in the Prime Minister's Office in the UK. The Prime Minister was in power through a coalition of political parties led by Labour. While this unit was formally a new one, there had been a number of policy shops in that office over the years. He knew that his assignment to develop a research budget for colleges and universities was a repeat of one that had occurred the last time the Labour Party had been in power. His predecessor had interpreted that assignment as requiring the development of a structured way of using information from colleges and universities based on criteria that emphasized research production rather than teaching. Each institution was asked to prepare standard statistical and narrative material for submission to central panels for assessment. The process was designed to reward and promote high quality efforts.

Williams knew that the process had not produced the results that his predecessor had expected. It led to decisions that gave resources only to the elite institutions. It led to the closing of departments and fields that emphasized teaching and not research. It was designed as a "rational" system for allocating funds without consulting interested organizations (such as the Association of University Teachers) and others who could probably anticipate the results. As a result, it generated criticism from Labour Party voters and led to Labour's loss of power. Williams did not know how to deal with that past experience. Budget staff liked to produce decisions based on data but he didn't want to repeat the problems, reactions and consequences of the past.

James Williamson was recently hired by a consortium of foundations that supported higher education programs for students from families who did not have the resources to pay for college or university for their children. Before assuming this position, he had worked for two of the 12 state agencies that received funds from the consortium. The two agencies were very different from each other and he realized that differences between them suggested that it was hard to generalize about these agencies. The environment of each was very different; the structure of the government, the composition of the population in the state, and the financial condition of the state made a difference in the way they used the funds.

Williamson's new job as director of the consortium required him to define expectations about the use of the funding. He thought that his past experience was very relevant but he was expected to define something at the centralized level. His instincts told him that traditional performance measurement reports wouldn't get at those conflicting expectations. But he wasn't sure whether a process approach that emphasized collaborative efforts would be acceptable to the board of his organization.

Is It Possible to Anticipate Uncertainty and Change?

As Chapter 4 suggested, policy analysts frequently face an environment that is both uncertain and always changing. Sometimes these shifts can be attributed to changes that emerge from the political environment (e.g., elections, change of leadership, crises). Others times they emerge from natural disasters or other unforeseen events. At any rate, they make predictability a scarce commodity. It is often hard for an analyst to invest in analytic activities that cover long stretches of time. For example, a multi-year evaluation may produce results that are available too far in the future; that can be a time when new decisionmakers may have come into the setting or other changes may have occurred. In other cases, changes may occur in the analyst's life that make long-term plans quite unpredictable.

Marjorie Benson *returned to the US Department of Health and Human Services from her maternity leave a year after the Trump administration had assumed power. She left her position in the Office of the Assistant Secretary for Planning and Evaluation at the end of the Obama administration and returned to a new political cast of characters who were committed to eliminating the Affordable Care Act, the policy she had worked on for the previous eight years. Her new supervisor was a political appointee who had worked on Capitol Hill for the Republicans during the Obama years.*

Before she left she had written a series of analytic memos that seemed to be totally irrelevant when she returned to the department. She had never anticipated the possibility that would happen despite the efforts in Congress to kill the program throughout the second Obama term. She is re-evaluating her career and attempting to figure out how she could continue her work on health policy in this new environment.

Reema Chatterjee *developed a career progression that seemed to fit her personal and professional interests. Her work at the IMF seemed to be fairly predictable and she and her husband had made a successful transition to life in the US. An offer of eligibility for a lifetime pension for both members of the family was an overture that she and her husband could not resist. They both had families in India who were aging and they also were concerned that their children were growing up without Indian roots. They assumed that they could start a consulting firm in Delhi that would draw on both of their competencies.*

Neither of them was ready for the changes that they faced when they returned to India. The historical commitments to independence and the role of the public sector seemed to have vanished. Religious conflict prevailed and the role of political controversy was difficult to avoid. Could they have predicted this?

Lisa Li *was tasked with an assignment from the Hong Kong Secretary of Education to develop a five-year strategic plan for the Hong Kong Education Bureau.*

While she had familiarity with strategic planning in her postings as an administrative officer in other settings, she soon found that this assignment was going to be very difficult. Strategic plans usually build on patterns from the past and present that can be extrapolated to the future. But she soon learned that wasn't the case in her current assignment. She found that projections were difficult to make for Hong Kong education because of two sets of uncertainty.

One set of uncertainties emerged from the changing political relationship between Hong Kong and the Chinese mainland. That had the potential of changing many aspects of the program, including requirements of instruction, the curriculum and relationships to the mainland's provinces. The second set of uncertainties emerged from the population changes within Hong Kong. That involved patterns of population from foreigners as well as individuals from the mainland. Both of these forces made her skeptical about the accuracy of a strategic plan that she might develop.

Another source of uncertainty stems from rules and schedules of players that are different from those of the expected client of the analysis. James Mason was concerned about the way that the State of North Carolina had defined the boundaries of its congressional districts. He had some ideas about what could be done to change those boundary lines but wasn't prepared for a decision by a panel of federal judges that struck down the state's existing map. That decision changed the environment for an alternate policy and Mason was trying to figure out how to deal with what might be called an opening regarding the issue. While the federal court was not really the formal client for his activity, it really defined the possibilities that might be available to him.

Is There a Type of Information That Documents Cultural Norms?

Policy analysts may find themselves in a situation where they face a conflict between budget or other quantitative information and information that stems from cultural or symbolic beliefs and norms. It is difficult to put the two types of information together.

Patrick Nonet was faced with such a dilemma when he took a job with the Canadian national government to examine the future of the existing bilingual language policy in the country. A native of French-speaking Quebec, he had been involved in the unsuccessful Quebec succession movement and election in 1995. He knew that increasingly a lower percentage of Canadians now use French as their native language. A decrease in these requirements was likely to reduce the national government's budget. But he also knew that Quebec residents viewed bilingual requirements as symbolic of their heritage and unique perspective. He wanted to include this argument in his role as the staff director of a Prime Minister's Commission that is charged with an examination of the future of the language policy but believed that it would be hard to convince non-Quebec residents or even the current prime minister who was from Quebec.

As a member of a multi-generation family that was involved in the coal industry, George Smith found it difficult to deal with current issues related to coal mining in West Virginia. He thought that advocates of reinvigorating mining as well as advocates of developing alternatives to mining didn't really understand the culture that was important to his family. He found it difficult to translate his feelings as well as those of his family into information that decisionmakers would understand. That unique culture and those family commitments were hard to describe.

What Kind of Information is Most Effective When the Analyst Wants to Play an Advocacy Role?

It is clear that some analysts approach the use of information in a way that is somewhat similar to the lawyers' definition of evidence. They begin with a preferred response to a policy problem and search for information that will help them make a case for that perspective. While that search may lead to some changes in a.final recommendation, it is quite different than the concern about neutrality that is found in more traditional research approaches.

Joyce Winter's long-term work in environmental issues in California was being attacked by the policies of the Trump administration. Although she knew that there would always be tension between a state role and that of the national government, the current situation seemed to erode the policy space available to the state to develop environmental regulations. In addition, the scientific community across the country was very concerned about the disregard that Washington had for research that justified the regulatory agenda.

She was close to retirement and wanted to make sure that whatever she chose to do would put her concerns on the policy agenda. She was considering several types of options: Creating a new advocacy organization, commissioning a study or book on the issues, or identifying prominent Californians who would be the leaders in such an effort.

Whatever she chose to do had to highlight the problem and draw on the arguments based on science for her position.

The Limits of Formal Data Systems

As was noted earlier in this chapter, data sources used by policy analysts are often developed for other purposes. As such, analysts may find that the existing information is not disaggregated or presented in categories that are useful to them. Two of the case studies used in this book illustrate this problem.

Renee Hernandez was hired by a consulting firm to continue work on a performance assessment of the Dallas School District. As she familiarized herself with the work of her predecessors, she realized that the data set they were using did not present the information in categories that represented the diverse composition of the school system. She thought this was important since there appeared to be different experiences for Hispanics, African Americans and Anglos as both students and teachers in the system.

It seemed that the past leadership of the school district had focused on issues involving African Americans in the system and gave little attention to the experience of Hispanics. She thought that would continue in the future if they continued to use the existing data set.

Marianne Williams had a similar experience. She worked for the Baltimore Police Department on their Performance-Stat effort. That performance assessment work seemed to be based on the attempt of the Mayor and city council to make sure that the police department was accountable to their political masters. That data system was organized around geographic dimensions related to the location of police headquarters. Those boundaries did not correspond to residential patterns that reflected racial and economic differences. Williams spent some time looking at past performance reports and found very little in the system that helped to explain the circumstances that had led to the death of Freddie Gray, an African American who died in police custody. That death led to demonstrations and riots by citizens in the affected districts. She thought that the data system that was used was a one-size-fits-all approach that wasn't sensitive to the location of the problems.

Limits of Data Produced by Research Activities

The dichotomy between policy analysis and policy research described by Vining and Weimer sometimes leads to a conflict between the two enterprises. *Ellen Winston chose to work in an advocacy organization that dealt with welfare policy issues. The office she worked in was called the policy analysis office; it seemed to encourage the staff to undertake research projects that they believed would be useful to the organization in its advocacy role. Those projects focused on issues that were likely to emerge within a year or two. She learned that her office and the lobbying office both reported to the same vice president of the organization; they also shared a common budget.*

Winston began to see that the research projects she proposed were not funded because the vice president chose to support projects that provided immediate information to the lobbying staff. She was told by a senior member of the staff that it was more important to focus on issues that were already on the agenda than on issues that had yet to emerge.

Ability of Information to Facilitate Bargaining and Trade-Offs

Some sources of information are structured in a way that determines whether alternative solutions to a policy issue are either true or false. When that type of information is presented to those involved in dealing with multiple players, multiple perspectives and other realities of the decision-making process, it may inhibit the bargaining and trade-offs that are required to come to a decision.

Jonathan Weston came into the US Department of Energy with a perspective that was well honed because of his past experience as the chair of a Government Affairs Committee of the Association of Windmill Manufacturers. He could document that perspective with data that indicated that the federal government was hurting the economic condition of the companies in his association. His staff exposed him to a range of issues and actors who had views that were different than those with which he was familiar. He realized that information would not facilitate reaching an agreement.

Similarly, Curtis Brown realized that his boss in the State of Virginia's Department of Corrections wanted to consider policy options that might include involvement of both the private sector and the public sector in the building of new prisons in the state. He didn't know how to deal with this complex assignment and felt that the information about the contributions of both sectors was actually contradictory and confusing. Should he present that information to advocates of public, private and mixed involvement? Should he meet with each group separately? And what information should he give them? Would that help them make a decision?

William O'Neill is a consultant who was contacted by a number of groups and individuals who are all concerned about the removal from the Australian Parliament of several elected members because they had dual citizenship in both Australia and another country. He was having difficulty focusing on the way that this very complex issues could be framed. He had decided that it could be viewed as a partisan political issue, an issue left over from Australia's colonial past, or an expression of current immigration policy. There was information available about each of these three definitions but it was extremely difficult to find ways to determine how to trade-off between elements in them.

Veronica Lopez is a physician who has become a policy analyst. She has worked in US federal agencies, international health bodies and a foundation concerned about global health issues. She is now on the staff of the World Health Association and has been asked to clarify the roles that are played by international health agencies (with membership of national representatives) and global health networks (whose activities involve a range of non-state organizations and approaches). She is attempting to identify ways that the two approaches could work together more effectively. It is not clear to her whether there are information sources that might assist her in this assignment or how she can deal with this conflict.

Conclusion

These examples (and probably many others) indicate the complexity of the information choice in policy analysis. Information clearly comes in many different forms, based on an array of assumptions about its collection and use. While the collection of research information can be costly in terms of time as well as resources, it is usually based on a set of principles that are linked to the values of the scientific method. That is not the case with information use and production in policy analysis. The presence of the client, the environment of uncertainty and change, and the ambiguities embedded in many policy problems make the choice of information sources challenging.

Note

1   Weiss also defined the information problem as resulting from three forces: Information, ideology and interests.

[handwritten notes:] policy analysis information research isn't like scientific research but might be taken as such

7 Criteria and Values

There is one element in the policy analysis field that has been maintained over the years despite the changes that have surfaced in the more than half a century since the field appeared as a profession. That element is a strong commitment (although not a universal one) by the analyst to provide alternative ways (or options) that the client might consider to address the policy problem. In that sense, the presence of choice grows out of the values of a democracy.

The choice could be between an alternative to "do something" about the issue and an alternative that simply gives the client an opportunity to decide to "do nothing" about it. But working on alternatives does provide the analyst with some creative space to think about different approaches to the problem. Weimer and Vining suggest that there are four sources for developing policy alternatives:

> (1) existing policy proposals; (2) generic policy solutions ...; (3) 'modified' generic policy solutions; and (4) custom-made solutions.... Although the particular technical, institutional, political and historical features of the problem may limit their direct applicability, the generic solutions can provide a framework for crafting and classifying more complex alternatives.
>
> (Weimer and Vining, 1992, p. 225)

As has been discussed in the earlier chapters of this book, many policy issues that have emerged in the twenty-first century are sui generis. They represent new developments within the society, are constantly changing, are a combination of policy problems, or stem from the addition of new players or new issues in the policy environment. They call out for approaches that might seem to be "out of the box" and often contain elements that are viewed as contradictory. Such situations make it difficult to use even highly sophisticated quantitative methodologies. Rather, they seem to be responsive to methodologies that rest on the development of logic systems that might include items that are difficult to quantify.

Two types of information might be included in these systems. One involves items that rest on the presence of more than one value. It is useful to rely on the classic economic categorization of *effectiveness, efficiency* and *equity* values since many policy issues involve goals that include two or even all three of these categories. Multiple and contradictory values are often found in contemporary policy issues. This is one of the main differences between the public and private sectors.

The second information source allows an analyst to devise criteria that represent four different categories of issues. Each of the categories often contains multiple and even conflicting desires. These are *cost* (different types of cost to different players); *effectiveness* (achieving the goal or goals of the policy); *political feasibility* (determining the response of the relevant actors and their motivations, strategies, resources and arguments); and *implementability* (focusing on the actor who has responsibility to implement the policy, the relationship between new responsibilities and existing work, staff capacity, resources available, time frame and leadership potential).

The items that emerge from each of these categories set the scene for trade-offs between alternatives. Not surprisingly the political feasibility items often provide a picture of the opportunities that might be created to establish trade-offs between different options. The more diverse the multiple players in a situation are the less likely it will be that any one perspective has the ability to play a veto role in the decision process. Clearly some criteria will be more important to some of the players but the weighting process does provide a way for the analyst to discuss priorities with their clients.

Multiple Criteria Analysis

Multiple Criteria Analysis is the technique that has been used by policy analysts to find ways to deal with complex policy issues that lack obvious information sources and seem to call for contradictory goals. Its definition in Wikipedia emphasizes its ability to deal with issues that are complex but require an approach that moves in a logical fashion.

In our daily lives, we usually weigh multiple criteria implicitly and we may be comfortable with the consequences of such decisions that are made based on only intuition. On the other hand, when stakes are high, it is important to properly structure the problem and explicitly evaluate multiple criteria. In making the decision of whether to build a nuclear power plant or not, and where to build it, there are not only very complex issues involving multiple criteria, but there are also multiple parties who are deeply affected by the consequences.

Multiple Criteria Analysis is a way to define the criteria that emerge from the cost, effectiveness, political feasibility and implementability categories and use them to make a systematic examination of each alternative that has been identified. Each of the four categories is likely to contain multiple criteria that define the complexity of the issue. For example, a cost category would likely include several items that reflect concern about cost to different players involved in the issue. Similarly, the effectiveness category might contain several items that express multiple goals and objectives of the policy or program. The political feasibility category also is likely to contain the perspectives of different players in the policy area or find a way to maximize support for the effort and minimize the opposition. Implementability – the last category – provides a way for the analyst to include implementation issues in the analysis (since that is often something that is not usually found in traditional policy analysis approaches).

Techniques of Weighting Criteria

There are a number of ways for analysts to express different weighting techniques. Often both clients and analysts find it easiest to use numerical weights to indicate which criteria are the most important. Providing a weight of, for instance, 1 to 10 would indicate that 10 is the most important while 1 is least important. The range can allow similar weights for different options. These will allow the analyst or the client to construct new approaches that emerge from these assessments which may (or may not) lead to a recommendation. Some analysts chose to weight options in rank order. In that sense, four options will always be ranked from one to four. Still others shy away from numerical assessments at all and use adjectives to label the importance of the criterion.

If a policy area is complex with multiple players, criteria and goals, an analyst might ask the players individually to provide a weight to each of the items. Those individual assessments can be tabulated to provide an aggregate assessment for the item.

Table 7.1 Criteria Analysis Framework

Families of Criteria	Option 1	Option 2	Option 3
Cost (Weight)			
Effectiveness (Weight)			
Political Feasibility (Weight)			
Implementability (Weight)			

It is not always useful to move to the aggregate assessment because it can mask the conflict that may be important to acknowledge.

Looking at the Cases for Criteria and Values

The cases that have been written for this book were developed because they raise issues that do not fit easily into the traditional policy analysis framework. In that sense, they are particularly challenging for both a policy analyst and that person's client (or clients). The comments that are included in this section of the chapter are meant to provide suggestions to policy analysts about possible ways to think about the complexity they may encounter. These comments are examples of promising ideas that may lead to the definition of criteria and options in situations drawn from across the globe. They also attempt to illustrate issues that are likely to arise for policy analysts who are at different stages in their careers and come to their assignments with a personal background, values and expectations. Similarly, clients in the cases also represent different values and expectations. I have tried to emphasize particular suggestions that may not have been obvious to the reader but may give them some ideas for future policy analysis assignments. The examples that follow are not exhaustive but are meant to be suggestive.

The examples that have been used in this volume illustrate a range of situations. Not only do they focus on classic issues related to the policy analysis field but also to new issues that are topical today. In addition, a number of the cases deal with issues related to a policy analyst's career decisions.

Margaret Trumball is a policy analyst at the European Commission in Brussels. Trumball's assignment deals with the development of a migration policy for the 28 members of the EU. Her formal client is the head of the policy analysis unit who is from Poland. She knows that there is significant difference between members' experience with the migration issue. Some are dealing with it as a crisis issue because of refugees entering the country; that has created both disruption and high costs for the country. Others are concerned about the potential of the issue coming across their borders. Still others have welcomed migrants who bring skills and experience to the country.

While officially she is reporting to the head of the policy analysis unit, she knows that different countries will come to the table with different expectations and problems.

She believes that it is important for her to think of her client as all of the members of the EU. While they all have the ability to vote on the issue, she thinks she cannot expect all of the countries to be concerned about the issue with the same level of intensity given their variable involvement in the issue. When she begins to define criteria she realizes that different members will emphasize different aspects of the issue. Some may focus on avoiding disruption, some on implementation issues and some on cost. And some countries will define its goals to minimize migration while others may welcome it if it takes particular directions.

In addition, Trumball's several month experience on the staff has shown her that her staff colleagues may approach the issue in different ways. Some of them have been on the staff for many years and seem to have been socialized to their positions in a way that is very similar to the staff culture she experienced at the United Nations. They rely on technical expertise and views of management largely drawn from British and French centralized systems. The newer staff who come from the former Soviet Union countries have a different view about management. They tend to bring expectations from their country to the positions. And few of the newer countries have been overwhelmed by the new migrants.

Even though this issue is of concern to other multinational organizations, she believes that the complexity of the problem within the European Commission is already overwhelming. She decides to limit her analysis to players and ideas within the organization. But she has decided that she does not want to include a recommendation in her analysis but rather provide the clients with alternatives that they will consider themselves.

James Williams is a budget analyst in the Prime Minister's Office in the UK. Williams is concerned about the goals of the policy program he is analyzing. His assignment is to develop a research budget for colleges and universities. This assignment is a repeat of an effort some years ago to allocate the funds for this program on a rational basis. It appears that the budget staff assigned to the earlier problem were traditional budget people who emphasized efficiency goals. They prepared an assignment for all of the colleges and universities that required them to base their research request on their ability to produce research. They did not consider the other major role of higher education: Teaching. In addition, they did not attempt to define differences between institutions and thus did not tailor expectations to meet the different needs of elite and non-elite bodies.

It was widely believed that the fiasco that followed the budget allocation based on this data had led to the Labour Party's loss of power because of criticism from the Association of University Teachers. While the Labour Party is now in power (but in a coalition government), Williams believes that his assignment is likely to be watched closely as the election date approaches.

Williams wants to develop a process that appears to be defensible but he also recognizes that the program needs to include more than efficiency values in its development. He thinks that the program's criteria for choice should also include effectiveness and equity objectives. That would provide information about the relationship between research and teaching and differentiate between types of institutions. He also wants to include an appeal process within his options, providing an institution with an opportunity to question the distribution proposed for them.

Majorie Benson is now a staff member in the Office of the Assistant Secretary for Planning and Evaluation in the US Department of Health and Human Services. She has just returned from maternity leave to find an office that was totally different from the one she left a year ago. Before she left she was one of the staff members who was assigned to develop the Affordable Care Act during the Obama administration. She had spent the first term of the Obama administration working on its formulation and adoption and the second term focusing on its implementation.

The election of Donald Trump and Republican control of Congress made dramatic changes that affected her job. Her boss was someone who moved from the Republican staff of the House of Representatives to a political appointment in HHS. She had some contact with him in the past and she knew that he did not believe that health services should be provided or supported by the federal government. That position was dramatically different than the one she espoused.

Benson clearly needed a job and with a new baby she and her husband only lived comfortably as a result of two salaries. Neither of them wanted to leave the Washington, DC area. She was very committed to the health policy field and felt that she had developed expertise in that area that she wanted to continue to develop. She had expected to continue her career inside the federal bureaucracy but now realized that she should expand her search beyond her *current position. She knew that health policy was a large complex field and there were likely to be other positions for a policy analyst who had her values and interests. But she needed to think about positions that might be possible and to let her professional acquaintances know of her interests and her personal values and concerns.*

She began her search by looking for health policy programs that hadn't been attacked by the Trump administration or had support from Republicans in Congress. She identified the committees and subcommittees in Congress that had jurisdiction over those programs. She also looked for programs that continued to have support from interest groups and non-profit organizations. Because the judiciary branch had been involved in decisions affecting health policy, she sought out law firms that were involved in health cases and which might need a health analyst on their staff. She decided to give her search six months to see what she could identify as possibilities. She realized that even individuals who have career positions may not escape the political environment's changes.

James Marlin is a staff member in the US Department of Agriculture. He had been involved in rural development policies for many years. During this period he realized that there were differences between the way that USDA defined "rural" and the way that other agencies and departments thought about rural citizens and their issues. If the federal government were to become involved in "rural development" policies it needed to acknowledge that "rural" did not only involve farming but involved education, infrastructure, economic development, housing, health and environmental issues. It also cut across levels of government, not simply the federal level.

For several decades Marlin had been working with mid-level career bureaucrats across both federal and state staffs. They met on a regular basis without the traditional governmental formalism. They realized that they had become a loosely defined network that served collectively as the client for their activity. It lacked formal accountability elements and had no separate budget, authority or legislation, or formal structure.

Marlin was concerned about the ability of the network to withstand changes in staff, retirements and political pressures from both Congress and the executive branch. He wondered whether it was possible for the group to move from informal relationships to a more formal status. Some of the staff had moved up the career line and it was difficult for them to protect their time to attend the meetings. But the relationships with members of state rural development councils gave federal staff an unusual opportunity to share views with a diverse group of state, local and non-government players.

Marlin thought it might make sense to put together a group of participants who were a part of the network and ask them to identify two things: First, options that could be considered that may include a combination of formal and informal approaches; and second, a listing of instances where the informal process prohibited the participants from achieving their desired activity. He thought that interim step might help him clarify the issue before him.

Patrick Nonet is a member of the staff of the Prime Minister's Commission on Language Policy. He has recently moved from a job with the provincial government of Quebec to the Canadian national government. He is close to retirement and has been known as one of the most visible advocates of the bilingual approach developed in the Official Languages Act of 1969 which required both French and English to be the official languages of Canada. The use of the French language alongside English was one of the main demands of French-speaking Canadians, especially those living in the Quebec province. It was believed that the French language requirement served to defeat the Quebec succession movement and election in 1995.

Nonet agreed to end his career by taking the position in the Canadian national government at the time when the current prime minister – a French speaker and the son of a former prime minister – was in power. There was also a perception in the country that there was a significant decline in the proportion of Canadians who were using French as their native language.

His experience during the succession movement years was quite painful and he was pleased that the issue seemed to have reduced political conflict in the country. At the same time, his personal values and experience made him quite uneasy about seeming to move away from the French–Canadian culture. He also knew that continuing the bilingual requirement created a significant financial cost for the Canadian national government. He thought that the situation illustrated a combination of both efficiency and equity values. It also was an important way of acknowledging the dimensions of Canadian federalism – a structure that provided discretion and authority to individual states in a number of policy areas.

Nonet approached his new position believing that he could be an advocate for options that would not be perceived as dramatic changes. At the same time, he thought it was important to maintain some of the symbolism of the culture. As a result, he has decided to offer options that indicate some incremental change that would save some money but not dramatically change the status quo. He realized that the time frame for his work will be affected by the timing of political campaigns in the country.

WANG Liping is on the staff of the President of the Peoples' Republic of China. Over the past few years he has been assigned to work on environmental issues and accompanied the President to the United Nations Framework Convention on Climate Change in Paris (the Paris Agreement) in 2015. While he began his involvement with the environmental issue as an international problem it became increasingly clear that it had significant domestic impacts inside China that vary in terms of effects on different provinces and industries. This variation involves both political and economic perspectives.

In addition, WANG has been asked to develop a policy position on this issue that reflects the three roles of the President – the administrative role as President, leader of the Communist Party and commander in chief of the military. He knows that each of the roles focuses on different aspects of an already complex issue.

He has put together an informal advisory group that will provide him with the views of a range of actors. Each of these actors has its own formal or informal think tank that should be able to articulate the concerns of their perspective. He has asked each member of the advisory group to prepare a position paper that outlines its own concerns as well as areas in which they might have either disagreement or agreement with other players. WANG knows that his choice of actors may be criticized but feels that this is one of the few ways for him to map the dimensions of the issue.

WANG knows that his request to the members of the informal advisory group could be risky for him in terms of his career. He was moving into an even more complex policy environment and hoping that the players he designated would find it both stimulating and helpful to learn about the way that others defined the values and criteria that were relevant to them. He even wondered whether they would be able to exchange information in a language that extended across their different cultures.

Joyce Winter is a well-known advocate of environmental policies that had emerged from the State of California. She has been concerned about the changes in this policy sector that have emerged from the Trump administration. For decades she has been a leader in the role that California has played nationally in this policy area. That role was one of acting as a pioneer in the US and providing a model for environmental policies that have become the basis for national programs. By contrast, the Trump administration has treated the reach of the California environmental programs as the problem to be addressed.

Her broad experience with the environmental policy sector has made her feel that the positions supported by the Trump administration do not represent the views of a majority of the American population. But the authority of the White House provides both influence and resources that are hard to match. Winter *believes that one of the strongest arguments that she can use to slow down these problems is to work with groups in society who want to avoid or minimize disruption in their current status.*

She has identified four groups that she thinks can assist her agenda. They are the auto industry; the scientific community; other states and their officials who share her agenda; and the global community. She could work with them individually or collectively. Some of them are already experiencing forms of economic and political disruption. She believes that all four groups have tried to make rational arguments and reach out to their traditional contacts but they have not been effective in even slowing down the Trump agenda.

The options she is considering involve different ways of organizing and publicizing the disruption argument. She believes that each of the groups can identify others who might join the collective strategy. She believes that this strategy is likely to receive public attention through a range of different tactics.

Renee Hernandez was hired by a consulting firm in Dallas to work on a contract to do policy analysis for the Dallas School District. Her MPP program at the LBJ School at the University of Texas had focused on performance assessment of schools in Texas with a large bilingual student body. She had an office in the school district and when she arrived discovered that the data system that was being used in Dallas did not contain disaggregated data that would provide information about Hispanic, African American and Anglo students and faculty. She also learned that the leadership in the school district was largely African American and they seemed to be able to bring other sources of information about their community to the decision process.

When she attended school board meetings she became more aware of the tensions within the district. She did not know whether the consulting firm which now employed her was responsible for designing the data system that was being used for the past performance measurement activity. As such she was reluctant to raise the issue with her immediate supervisor from the firm. She had extensive tuition loans to repay and was concerned about maintaining her position. In addition, her conversations with school district staff suggested that there was racial and ethnic tension within the staff. An election for school board members was scheduled within the next 18 months but she did not know how that election might affect her work.

Hernandez decided to pursue an incremental strategy to deal with the limits of the data. The options that she was considering all focused on ways to modify and expand the data system. She decided that it made more sense for her to keep the problem inside the system and thus did not want to contact either state or national actors who might be interested in this situation. Instead, she decided to find ways to modify the information source to produce disaggregated information by race and ethnicity. Her criteria involved minimizing disruption, protecting her position and finding ways to educate her co-workers about the limitations of the current system. She also considered identifying other districts with similar problems and learning about other possibilities.

James Mason is a native North Carolinian who has been an active participant in politics in the state. He had been active in the state NAACP organization and worked closely with the North Carolina Legislative Black Caucus. Mason had been a member of the campaign staff of the current governor, a Democrat who was supported by a majority of the African Americans active in the state's political world. Over the past few years he has been very interested in the boundary lines establishing North Carolina's congressional map. A panel of federal judges just recently blocked a congressional map because of a partisan gerrymander that minimized the impact of African American voters. It appeared that court opinion represented an argument that many of his colleagues expected to lead to significant changes.

He has been offered a job by the Governor but was conflicted about the career path that he should take. Mason's past interests involved efforts that linked race and politics within the state. He wasn't sure whether he had reached a juncture in the road where he would have to choose between the two approaches. He was still quite young and didn't expect to be someone who would be able to move back and forth between the two issues easily.

He did realize that focusing on the gerrymander aspect of the issue would require him to develop technical knowledge about the process. It was his view that someone who was neither a lawyer or a gerrymander expert might have trouble being considered for such a job. He couldn't be assured that a job that he was qualified for would open any professional development doors. But he also knew that moving to the Governor's Office as a former campaign member of staff might limit his involvement in the process of drawing new district lines.

Mason tried to sit down to list the various criteria that he would use to choose between options. That was not easy. He also realized that there might be a third option that might be appropriate for him to consider – to think about enrolling in an academic program that would provide him with new skills and invest in his future. He wasn't sure what to do next.

Ellen Winston has been working for one of the major advocacy groups on welfare issues in its policy analysis unit. She was thrilled to land a job in that organization since it represented the policy issue she had been working on for some years. Her colleagues in the office were people who were well known and were the authors of books that she had on her book shelves. She had been *especially attracted to the organization because it seemed to link both policy research and policy analysis in its work.*

After about six months she realized that both her policy analysis unit and the lobbying unit reported to the same vice president of the organization. As such, they actually competed with one another for funds and attention in the organization. She found that the lobbying staff (called the legislative unit) usually made a case for its agenda based on political realities and a short time frame. By contrast, her office took a longer time perspective and approached issues more like researchers than "quick and dirty" policy analysts.

She did know that there were differences between policy research and policy analysis but working on topical issues that were likely to receive public attention would also assist the organization in its fund raising. She hadn't really considered other issues and differences that might emerge. In fact, she wasn't completely sure which form would be more personally satisfying to her since she was more familiar with the research culture than lobbying.

Winston thought there were at least three options available to her. She could stay where she was. She could look for another job that focused on policy research. Or she could stay where she was but look for ways to work with the staff of the lobbying organization on specific projects. She found it useful to list the criteria that she would use to choose between the three possibilities. She also realized that coming congressional elections might affect the organization's emphasis on their lobbying efforts.

Colleen Hendricks works for the New York City Housing Authority and is a midcareer policy analyst dealing with low-income housing programs. She is a native New Yorker from a family that has been involved in activities dealing with social problems experienced by both racial and ethnic minorities. She has worked at the Housing Authority for most of her career and has become very familiar with both government and non-profit organizations involved in this set of issues.

Her most recent work has involved an analysis of the sources of the housing supply for this population. Given the size of the New York City population she expected that the city would be able to draw on the sources that were controlled by various players at the state level. Her analysis indicated something quite different. Her conclusion was that the decision processes used by both the Governor's Office and the state legislature reflected the interests of small town and rural residents. She was surprised that even governors who were natives of New York City did not seem to focus on this pattern.

Hendricks could not completely separate her professional agenda from her personal realities. She was a classic New Yorker and had no idea what it would be like to live in Albany, separated from her family and long-term friends. She knew that the cost of living was lower in the capitol but probably the pay levels were also lower. Perhaps most importantly, she acknowledged that she did not understand the reasons behind the state level decision-making. Were there reasons for these processes that were rational and clearly difficult to modify?

She seemed to have several options available to her. First, she could stay where she was but try to cultivate contacts in Albany. Second, she could begin to look for openings at the state level and explore them. Third, she could move from a government role (in either state or local agencies) to an NGO involved with the issue. She needed to spend time defining the criteria she would use to choose among these three.

George Smith recently completed an MPP in public policy from the University of West Virginia. He was the first person in his family to complete a graduate degree. He was also the first male member of the family who did not work in a coal mine by the time he reached voting age. His grandfather was one of the leaders of the United Mine Workers Union and had been involved in the creation of the health system established to provide medical services for families of union members working in the mines.

He knows that it is time for him to look for a job. But he finds himself quite confused about that situation. Should he stay in West Virginia? How can he deal with the position of some members of his family who supported Trump during the 2016 election because the candidate argued for the reinvigoration of the coal industry? At the same time, how can he ignore the critics of Trump's position who believe that environmental concerns justify the end of the coal industry?

Smith finds himself surrounded by people who do not acknowledge the contributions that the past workers and owners of the coal mines had made to the state and its citizens. He watched his friends leave the state because they did not see possibilities in either education opportunities or jobs. But he felt that leaving would violate the inheritance of change that he received from multiple generations of his family.

He had been attracted by recent efforts by the state teachers union to increase funding for teachers and educational programs. Their demonstrations reminded him of the stories that his grandfather told about picketing in the past.

He tried to use some of his analytical skills to lay out the alternatives that might be available to him. He realized that he wanted to make a choice that met his family values, his personal future and gave him an opportunity to use his education. He listed the following options: (1) leave West Virginia for a neighboring state where job opportunities seemed to be present. (2) apply for a job in the West Virginia state government. (3) identify people involved in the West Virginia Teachers Union to see whether there were possibilities in that sector.

Marianne Williams just completed her third year working for the Baltimore Police Department on their Performance-Stat effort. She started her full-time job (moving from an internship) immediately after completing her MPP at the University of Maryland. She was very pleased to move into that permanent position because the effort in the Baltimore Police Department had received a lot of positive attention from the criminal justice and public management community. Both the Mayor and the city council told the public about the complete information they were collecting about the performance of the police department.

As time went on, however, there was more criticism of those performance measurement efforts than praise. And the death of Freddie Gray (an African American who died in police custody) became what was known as a "focusing event" in the city. She avoided talking about her job to her friends. But she was puzzled. Why were the conditions that seemed to have sparked the police action missing from the performance information she had been collecting?

She spoke to many people in the African American neighborhoods and identified two problems that she thought had led to the demonstrations and despair she heard. The first problem stemmed from the expectations and perspective of the Mayor and city council. They were looking for information that described city-wide patterns of behavior rather than data that indicated differences across the city that might have resulted from diverse populations and very different settings. They believed that one-size-fits-all for the police sector, despite the differences in the communities. She noticed that the Maryland Governor's Office was silent about these developments and was puzzled by the changes that might occur during the coming election year.

The second problem became clearer to her when she went back to her notes from her public management class. She hadn't remembered that there was a literature about something called "street level bureaucracy." That described staff in a bureaucracy that weren't located in a central office but rather in the streets where the civil servants have direct contact with members of the general public.

It seemed to Williams that the problem she was facing had been created by the combination of the two realities. But she wasn't sure whether she was at a point in her career that provided her with a position and adequate authority to modify these practices.

She clearly needed some colleagues who shared her views and her diagnosis of the problem.

She thought that there were several pathways that she should explore. First, she needed to identify other people in the Baltimore area who would become her colleagues. They could come from the NGO community, the African American community or higher education. Those individuals might have projects or ideas that were similar to hers and they, too, were feeling very isolated from those with formal authority.

Second, those conversations might have uncovered possible job opportunities for her.

Third, she might consider returning to school, enrolling in a PhD program that would allow her to focus on the situation, write a dissertation about it and define her role as an academic. Or fourth, she could stay in her current job and make suggestions about the different forms of data that would be collected in the future.

Jonathan Weston had been the chair of a government affairs committee of the Association of Windmill Manufacturers and recently moved to a political appointment in the US Department of Energy. He moved into his new position easily. He was familiar with many of the staff based on his earlier activities and they also knew of his perspectives regarding policies that he viewed as a regulatory burden on the private sector. Both he, the existing staff and his old colleagues seemed to have assumed that he would continue his private sector views. They all expected the continued development of a conflictual situation even though Weston was now inside the system.

After several months in his new job, serving as the client for career staff analysts, he began to see that the regulatory measures that he had opposed in the past may actually be appropriate for the public sector role. That occurred slowly as he worked with the career officials. He realized that his past perspective on many issues did not expose him to the perspective of players that he had not considered in the past. He hadn't acknowledged that many decisions involved other players within the Energy Department (who were involved in budget, legislative and other management decisions) as well as other federal agencies (such as EPA and the State Department). He also realized that there were many different interest groups involved in his issues who did not always agree with one another.

In fact, he began to think of the concept of regulation as much more complex than he had assumed when he was involved from the outside. He was very surprised when several members of the career staff praised him for "going native." He wasn't sure whether that characterization would follow him outside the *organization. Should he try to work invisibly inside the organization? How would he deal with his colleagues from the outside?*

Reema Chatterjee retired from the staff of the IMF after 25 years and returned to India to start a new chapter in her family's life. Both she and her husband were able to claim eligibility for lifetime pensions: She from the IMF and he from the World Bank. Although they regularly visited their families in India, they both felt that their parents were aging and their children were growing up without Indian roots.

They both thought that their experience at the bank and the IMF would provide them with contacts and expertise that could be transferred to Indian situations. They envisioned opening up a consulting firm once they were settled.

The move to India was complex. Housing prices were higher than she had expected. Her children were in their last years of high school and focusing on applying for universities in both the US and Canada. The children found the transition to India very difficult.

Chatterjee herself was shocked by the changes that had occurred in Indian society over those 25 years. Gandhi's influence had faded. The government's role had shifted to supporting the development of the private sector. Both religious and political conflict affected her day-to-day life. She found it difficult to figure out where she belonged in a society that still contained the expectations associated with the caste system.

While she knew that her earlier expectations were not realistic she wasn't sure how to deal with the situation. She did not want to leave her aging parents. She was apprehensive about her ability to develop clients for a consulting firm. She realized that the experience in the IMF and the World Bank might be easily translated into consultancies for both organizations. She and her husband could live in Delhi but work on projects in other countries. But she didn't know whether that was simply a way to avoid the problem but experience a difficult life style. They could also explore potential jobs in the NGO community in India as well as state governments. What were their options?

Curtis Brown is a staff member in the Virginia Department of Corrections. The secretary of the department has asked him to take the lead on a study that will determine whether a new prison in urban northern Virginia will be planned and operated by the private sector or the public sector. The issue has received attention because of past overcrowding in the state's existing system and also because of complaints by family members that prisoners from northern Virginia are placed in institutions in rural areas that are far away from their families, *limiting their ability to visit them. There is a pending legal complaint against the department that might surface at any time.*

Brown is overwhelmed by the complexity of the assignment. He believes that while the secretary is the "official" client, he has to think about a wide range of actors who are awaiting his report. He knows that there are vocal advocates for two different approaches to the issue: One represents private sector groups who want to build and/or run the new prison and the second represents the state government staff who also see themselves as responsible for both building and running the facility.

He also has tried to find a way to compare the strengths and weaknesses of both approaches. Brown has found it difficult to deal with the uncertainty found in the lurking role of the court system and the prison advocacy system. He also knows that a state like Virginia is likely to push the decision upward, probably to the desk of the Governor.

He is puzzled by this assignment. He is not familiar with the experience of other states who have tackled similar situations. Does the literature on this issue suggest that there are accepted but different approaches? What should he expect in terms of the overcrowding issue since the national data indicates a reduction in prison overcrowding?

Should he think about the building decision separately from the decision about who will run the facility? Do the competencies of the public and private sectors always compete with each other or are there times when they can complement one another? Is there some way that he could organize a demonstration effort that would indicate the response of both groups? Should he try to create an advisory board that represents different players and different perspectives? Would that create more conflict than he now expects?

He realized that he hadn't considered the possible impact of coming elections on his options. He knew that there was often conflict between the state government and local governments on one hand and a possible impact on the state of federal support for prison policies.

James Williamson has been recently hired by a consortium of foundations that supports higher education programs for low-income students in approximately 12 states.

While he is new to this job, he is quite familiar with its activities. Over the past 15 years he has been employed by two of the state agencies that received funds from the consortium. The consortium is 20 years old and made up of seven different foundations that support higher education programs. He was well known to the board of the consortium because he was a senior staff member in one of the states and director of the staff in another staff. His assignment as director of the consortium requires him to define expectations about the use of the consortium's funding.

Williamson's client group is actually very complex. The consortium has a board that is made up of representatives of each of the different foundations. It also has to deal with the policies of the higher education programs in each of the states, both the officials in the state and the organizations that are advocates for higher education. Through his experience over the years Williamson has become very aware of differences in the structure of the state government, the demographic composition of the state and the financial conditions in the jurisdiction.

Williamson believes that the diversity of the states would elicit strong opposition for a one-size-fits-all model for all of the programs. At the same time, he knows that states are sensitive to back-door deals that suggest one state is being held to less stringent requirements than another. He believes that whatever he does should be achieved collaboratively with the involvement of the state grantees as well as the groups represented in the client category. He also thinks that the 20-year experience of the consortium will provide the basis for an analysis of all the types of approaches that have emerged over these years.

His preliminary alternatives include: (1) the development of a demonstration effort in one state; (2) the creation of an advisory board that includes state representatives and board members; and (3) asking program participants to analyze the list of approaches to determine their assessment of which ought to be used.

William O'Neill is a consultant in Canberra, Australia. He is known for his willingness to take on jobs that others think are not doable. A small group of citizens came to him because they are concerned about the removal of several elected members from Parliament because they had dual citizenship in both Australia and another country. These parliamentarians were removed because of a requirement in Section 44 of the Australian constitution.

After his first conversation with these citizens, O'Neill realized that framing the policy problem was going to be extremely difficult. Not only did the potential clients represent very different perspectives on the situation (some were lawyers, some political activists and some represented immigration advocates) but they had very different time frames for responding to the issue. But they were all very concerned about the removal of these elected officials.

He began to think of the problem as an onion. He could peel off one layer and another quite different set of issues appeared. The first layer was that of partisan political issues; the removal of some of the parliamentarians challenged the current coalition that was in power. But beyond that, he came to believe that all of the other issues that surfaced had resulted from Australia's colonial past with England. Even though Australia had achieved its identity as a separate country at the turn of the twentieth century, its role in the British Commonwealth did not always suggest a traditional level of political autonomy. During the early years of its independence (until 1949) Australians could only hold the status of British citizens and experienced limitations on citizenship based on past British practices.

In the post-World War II period, the Australian population grew and the concept of multiculturalism became the norm replacing restrictions based on racial and ethnic differences. One analysis of the issue indicated that Australia's citizenship legislation has been amended over 30 times. Immigration issues have continued to be a problem as migrants have tried to land on Australia's shores.

O'Neill knew that this loose array of individuals was not really a formal group even though the individual members were well known. Should he think about limiting the scope of the problem before he tried to create some sort of an organization? Or should he try to gather the individuals together to create a temporary group that could share its expectations about the issue?

Lisa Li is an Administrative Officer in the Hong Kong Government who has been recently assigned to the Hong Kong Education Bureau. She has been given an assignment by the Secretary of Education that involves the development of a five-year strategic plan for the bureau. She had been assigned a similar task in another Hong Kong government office a few years earlier and evidently her current assignment was based on that experience.

Her first instinct when she arrived was to identify data sources that could be used for the assignment. Her belief was that strategic plans are based on longitudinal information that indicate patterns of development over time. In this case she approached her assignment believing that most agencies develop strategic plans based on the projection of population patterns but rely on past patterns as the basis for the new data.

But she began to realize that the uncertainty about future developments was not simply based on population patterns. Rather, it developed as a result of the changing political relationship between Hong Kong and the mainland of China. The newspapers were full of accounts of new ways that the mainland was limiting the autonomy of Hong Kong following the decision of the UK government to hand over Hong Kong to the People's Republic of China effective in 1997. The impact of that political change is unknown but it is possible that the Central Government may require Hong Kong to move its educational system closer to that found on the mainland. That could include requirements that deal with sensitive ideological differences between the two systems. Among these issues are the language of instruction, the curriculum and the relationship between Hong Kong and nearby provinces on the mainland.

Li also realized that this uncertainty has affected the population changes that have occurred within Hong Kong. That relates to the movement of people from the mainland to Hong Kong as well as the number of international families who have moved to Hong Kong for business reasons.

She is becoming increasingly convinced that her expertise in strategic planning will not prepare her for this assignment. She doesn't know the views of the Secretary for Education about the political situation. Should she try to clarify the situation by discussing it with her supervisor? Should she treat the assignment as a bureaucratic requirement that needs to be addressed? Should she organize her work around different scenarios that might be likely to emerge? Who should she discuss her dilemma with?

Veronica Lopez, MD, recently joined the staff of the World Health Organization (WHO). She is a pediatrician who specialized in infectious diseases but has spent much of her career as a policy analyst dealing with health issues. She started working for the US Centers for Disease Prevention and Control (CDC) but soon moved to the Pan American Health Association (PAHO). Her focus on Latin America took her to the Gates Foundation where she became aware of the power and potential of global health networks. During her tenure at the Gates Foundation she became aware of a tension between the efforts of international health structures (who operate through formal national and international structures) and the global health networks (whose activities involve a range of non-state organizations and approaches).

At the Gates Foundation Lopez became aware of what she termed a "gulf" between those who had expertise in major health problems (the networks) and those who had formal authority to deal with those problems. She had conversations with various players in the international health field and accepted an offer from the WHO to join their staff to clarify the role that each of the groups played and how they defined their audiences.

She was quite visible in the international health community and a number of people perceived her to be playing a combination of both analyst and client roles. She began her activity with several assumptions. She thought that the structure and formalism of groups like the WHO made them particularly sensitive to the political pressures that emerged from the nearly 200 member countries. At the same time, she observed that the WHO regularly relies on experts not affiliated with countries for consultation and formal recommendations.

She began her work by acknowledging that the WHO plays different roles. It establishes norms for its members; it enforces those norms as a regulator; it plays a research and development role by supporting research and pilot projects; and it provides a forum that would involve both official organizations such as WHO and non-official networks and creates a setting for them to share information. She observed that both groups seemed to organize themselves in smaller clusters based on specific subjects and diseases. Her hunch was that there may be some areas that are more "ripe" for collaboration than others. She also knew that the networks involved researchers who were at the cutting edge of many health issues and didn't want to lose their visibility.

She was convinced that her assignment required her to be sensitive to the process that she would use to make recommendations for collaboration in policy adoption and implementation. But she wasn't sure how to structure the next steps. Should she create an advisory committee? Should she work with each of the two groups separately? Should she focus on one or two subject areas and treat them as pilot efforts?

Conclusions

Each of these cases provides a preliminary perspective on the next steps that might be taken by either the analyst or the client. In most of the cases the challenge is to the analyst to move ahead. But all of the cases illustrate four realities: First, that policy problems are likely to be complex; second, that cultural and global differences are relevant; third, that it is important to be sensitive to differences in the stage of the analyst's career; and fourth, that it is valuable to think about the personal values and past experiences of both the client and the analyst.

8 A Check List

This chapter provides a check list which can serve as a structure for developing a policy analysis that meets some of the characteristics that have been emphasized in this book. This check list is meant to be useful in dealing with the complex issues raised more frequently during the twenty-first century than may have been encountered in the past. These are not policy problems that have clear clients, agreed upon goals, accessible data and seemingly appropriate analytic approaches. And – perhaps most importantly – they are problems that are expressed in different political structures and systems.

It is my hope that this array of questions will be useful in different settings across the globe. The cases that have been used to illustrate the challenges found in today's policy analysis activity are meant to acknowledge the diversity of clients that a contemporary policy analyst is likely to confront. These cases also illustrate the complicated relationship between the analyst's personal values and expectations and the demands of providing advice to various types of clients.

The case examples are drawn from both US and global settings and, as such, provide attention to the impact of the public sector structure, culture and political process on the policy analysis process. While there is no "right" answer to these items and issues, this list provides students of policy analysis with a way to anticipate possible problems and find ways to develop approaches that fit the reality of the diverse policy environments.

The check list items follow the structure of this volume. The list begins with issues related to clients and moves to analysts. It then moves to items that relate to the complexity of the policy environment and then to the policy issue itself. Information and evidence follow and the list concludes with items dealing with criteria and values.

Not all of these items are appropriate or relevant to someone beginning a policy analysis assignment. But the presence of a check list can help an analyst raise issues that are likely to be important to the policy analysis task.[1]

Clients

What is the client(s)'s authority base?

What is their past involvement with the issues at hand?

Are they new to the issue(s)?

What is their reputation within the organization?

What constrains them within the organization?

What political and value conflicts exist within the organization?

What has brought the policy problem to the table?

What are the assumptions about the causes of the policy problem?

Did the clients have past experience with the analyst?

Was contracting out a part of that past experience?

What assumptions does the client(s) have about the policy analysis process (the analyst, the techniques used)?

Policy Analysts

What is their background (experience and training)?

What skills do they bring to the assignment (political vs. technical skills)?

How do they define differences between policy research and policy analysis?

What personal values do they bring to the issues at hand?

At what stage of their career are they now?

What are their future career plans?

In what organizational setting are they placed?

What is their past relationship to the client(s)?

What assumptions do they have about the causes of the policy problem?

Do they approach the issue as a technical or a political problem?

What assumptions do they have about the analytic tools that are available?

What do they define as success (both substantively and in terms of process)?

The Environment

Who are the main players in the policy map?

Why were they included?

Have they been involved in similar issues in the past?

Are they inside or outside the formal decision-making environment?

What are their concerns?

What are the areas of conflict?

Have there been past trade-offs between players?

What is their involvement in the process?

If you decide not to include specific players why did you make that decision?

What is the structure of decision-making (centralized, federalized, networks)?

What are the different roles of the actors (resource controllers, those with authority, those with influence)?

Role of constituents?

Role of clients?

What is the nature of the environment (turbulent, uncertain, predictable)?

What causes that environmental type (elections, conflict, lack of resources)?

What is the client(s)'s span of authority (legal, shared with other agencies, legislative branch, courts)?

What are the changing values or cultural norms that affect the issue?

What is the background and role of the staff (professions, education, roles)?

What is the role of interest groups? Who are they? Areas of conflict?

What are their political links? Do they share authority?

The Issue Itself

Is this an issue that has emerged in the past?

How is the issue framed? Is this similar to framing in the past?

What players and issues are built into the framing process?

What are the major dimensions of the issue?

Is it possible to define either or both of the outcomes or outputs of the issue?

Are there specific cultural or historical attributes of the issue?

How did the issue emerge? Was it predictable (e.g., windows opening) or emergent (e.g., focusing event)?

At what stage of the policy process does it occur (agenda setting, formulation, adoption, implementation, evaluation)?

What are the policy conflicts that are built into the issue?

Is the analysis designed to educate the client(s)?

Is the analysis designed to make a recommendation to the client? If not, why?

Information and Evidence

What kinds of information are being used? About problem, about current policy situation, other settings, political intelligence, academic work, mobilize support, as a warning system, description of ideas for new strategies and procedures?

What information appears to be available? Any restrictions on its use?

Is information characterized as objective, subjective, formal, informal?

Do you start the analysis with existing data systems rather than information about the policy problem?

Is there a definition of difference between analysis and research?

Who produced the information and who paid for it?

How would you characterize the information producer (journalist, social scientist, advocate)?

How is the concept of "evidence" defined (to make choice, to justify solution, other)?

Is the information sensitive to cultural norms?

How to deal with multiple goals of a policy? With uncertainty and change?

Is information used to help create bargaining situations and trade-offs?

Criteria and Values

Is there acknowledgment that the client(s) have a choice in this situation?

How did the analyst create alternative ways to deal with the policy problem (e.g., speak to others, look at past information)?

What was the source of these alternatives (e.g., past experience, existing proposals, positions attached to different players)?

What are the predominant values built into the policy problem (e.g., efficiency, equity, effectiveness)?

How have multiple and conflicting values been acknowledged in the problem?

Where did the criteria come from? Are they attached to specific players? Who defined them?

How have the specific criteria within the families of criteria been defined? Is there definitional conflict within the families as well as between the families?

Have different weights been given to specific criteria? Who provided them?

Has the analyst created these definitions and weights with others (e.g., the client(s), outside players)?

Did the use of the criteria analysis format lead to trade-offs between values and players?

Overall Assessment

What were the most difficult questions to answer? Why?

What would you do differently as a result of this process?

Note

1 This concept of a check list was influenced by Atul Gawande's work (Gawande, 2011) on check lists in the health field.

Case Studies

Marjorie Benson entered the US federal government through a fellowship available to graduates of public policy (and related) graduate programs. Her MPP in public policy prepared her for a position in the Office of the Assistant Secretary for Planning and Evaluation in the US Department of Health and Human Services. She had spent the last eight years (the entire Obama administration) working on health policy issues. Most of those efforts were affected by the passage of the Affordable Care Act (ACA) during the first Obama term.

Because she was on maternity leave during the first year of the Trump administration, she had not experienced the dramatic changes that were attached to the change of administration. She returned to a staff that had new political leadership who were committed to finding a way to dramatically change the program that she had advocated. She wasn't sure how the remaining Assistant Secretary of Policy and Evaluation (ASPE) health staff were dealing with these changes but she didn't want to jeopardize her job. Ironically, the Deputy Assistant Secretary named by the Trump administration had spent the first few years of his career working in ASPE before he joined the Republican staff of the House Ways and Means Committee. As a result, Benson knew him, albeit superficially.

It was clear to her that the Health Deputy Assistant Secretary would measure his success in terms of the demise of the ACA. He was not interested in expanding coverage of programs to individuals who were currently not covered. He did not agree with her belief that health services should be viewed as a public responsibility rather than an area largely of private sector responsibility.

Benson thought that she had several choices that were available to her. She could accept the assignments that the Health Deputy Assistant Secretary gave her and define her role as a neutral civil servant who accepted the perspective of the party in power.

She could find areas of health policy that were supported by (or at least not opposed) by the Trump administration and focus on them. They would likely slip through the cracks since they didn't really touch the broader strategies. She might focus on efforts such as rural health programs and community-based health centers that did garner support from Republicans in Congress because of the need for health services in those congressional districts.

Alternatively, she could play the role of a "guerilla" in the government and feed information that countered the administration's policy agenda to groups and individuals who shared her values. Or she could look for another job.

Curtis Brown has been tasked with developing a plan for building new prisons in the state of Virginia. The state has experienced prison overcrowding over the past few years. It has been sued by prison advocacy groups and is attempting to avoid further litigation that could narrow its ability to define its own response to the problem. If a court issues a ruling on the problem, the state may not have control over the issue. Thus it wants to take pre-emptive action. At the same time, the state continues to face a tight budget.

The Governor's Office has received extensive public reaction to the issue. The Governor has asked the Secretary of the State Department of Corrections to develop an analysis that will help him make the decision. While there are very different perspectives on it, almost all of the public responses call for the building of a new prison in urban northern Virginia. Even though the population has grown in that part of the state, most of the current prisons are in rural areas. There are also groups that are encouraging the state to try something new in the design and management of prisons, looking to bring technology to the proposed prison.

There are at least two different views about this situation. One group of individuals sees this new prison as an opportunity to contract its design and management to the private sector. They favour privatizing the facility and operating it through a contract with a private organization. The other group believes that the facility should be controlled by the State Department of Corrections and want to keep this development inside the current system where the department would design and manage the institution.

Curtis Brown feels as if he is caught between two very different approaches. He believes that he needs to compare the situations that each is likely to confront. The private sector advocates will look at this issue as a way of privatizing the process. The public sector advocates will emphasize what can be done by running the process within the Department of Corrections. His comparison will also include an analysis of the other actors involved in the system.

He believes that a third perspective could be developed that combines attributes for both. He has decided to try this but knows he will have to satisfy both sets of actors.

He is attempting to construct a set of options for his client. He is not clear whether he should separate the two functions (designing the institution and managing it when it is built) or try to satisfy both perspectives in all of the process.

For the past 25 years **Reema Chatterjee** had been working for the International Monetary Fund (IMF) on projects dealing with infrastructure development. A citizen of India, Chatterjee joined the IMF on assignment from the Indian Administrative Service (IAS). After completing her IAS training and placement in the state of Rajastan, she had been sent to the US to complete a PhD in economics. She was about to return to India when she learned about the opening at the IMF dealing with the policies that were the subject of her doctoral dissertation.

Chatterjee was hired and found the IMF position stimulating and fascinating. She was based in Washington, DC but spent more than half of her time traveling to projects in a range of countries around the globe. Her colleagues were drawn from similarly diverse backgrounds. She saw herself as an international civil servant who roamed the globe.

During those 25 years, Chatterjee married an Indian who worked at the World Bank, purchased a house in the Washington suburbs, and had two children who attended American schools and identified as Americans. But as the years passed, both she and her husband found that they missed their families in India and were concerned that their children were growing up without Indian roots.

Both Chatterjees found that they were eligible for lifetime pensions from their organizations. Those pensions are payable at age 50 with a minimum of three years of service. The pensions were fairly generous and would allow the family to live comfortably in Delhi, India's capital. They each thought that it would be possible for them to develop consultantcy work, drawing on their past contacts.

The move to India was very complex. Housing prices were higher than she expected. Her children were entering university. They were applying to US and Canadian schools and weren't really focused on living in India. Her contacts from her IAS days were located around the country and were also retired. They didn't provide the contacts for work that the Chatterjees had expected.

Chatterjee really was shocked by the changes that had occurred in Indian society over those 25 years. The values attached to Indian independence had eroded. Not only was the society worshiping the gods of the private sector but Gandhi's concern about eliminating the remainder of the caste system didn't seem to be viewed as important. And the conflict between Hindus and Muslims in society seemed to be much stronger than she remembered. Politically, the strength of the

Congress party had diminished and state-specific political parties created a much more fragmented political culture.

Both Chatterjees found this set of developments very difficult to deal with. Should they try to use their past experience to work with nongovernmental organizations that shared their values? Or should they try to develop a consulting practice that worked at the margins? Should they even consider leaving India again?

Colleen Hendricks identified herself as a classic New Yorker. She grew up in Manhattan in a family that was always present at demonstrations dealing with social problems experienced by both racial and ethnic minorities. When she graduated from Bronx High School of Science (one of the elite public institutions in the city) she competed for and was chosen as an Urban Fellow and attended Baruch College for both her undergraduate and graduate degrees.

Her interest in housing issues led her to take a position with the New York City Housing Authority. She became familiar with the programs available in the city (sponsored by both city government and non-profit organizations) to increase the supply of housing for low-income residents. She worked in the agency for five years and while she was viewed as an exemplary staff member she began to realize the fiscal and authority limitations on her ability to really address the housing supply problem.

She saw that a number of programs were available that were controlled by the New York state government. Some of them were created and funded by the federal government and implementation was given to the state government to decide who would receive those resources. It seemed to Hendricks that the allocation of those funds was decided by the Governor as well as the state legislature. Despite the size of the New York City problem, neither of those two bodies seemed to be interested in changing the criteria they were using to allocate the funds.

In addition, she began to see that the picture of the problem that was contributing to her concern stemmed from the way that the New York state Legislature (particularly the Assembly) was structured to reflect the problems that were defined by small town and rural communities. In addition, even though New York state governors were often from New York City and its environs, they did not seem to reflect the concerns that motivated her.

Hendricks felt that she was at a crossroads. Should she stay in New York City or should she take a job in Albany? Was her diagnosis of the problem accurate and, if so, could she do something to change the way that decisions were made? Should she consider working on the issue from an organization outside of government? She was confused about those alternatives.

Renee Hernandez recently graduated from the LBJ School of Public Affairs at the University of Texas. She was hired by a consulting firm in Dallas that had a contract to do policy analysis for the Dallas School District. Her academic work at the LBJ School had focused on performance assessment of schools in Texas with a large bilingual student body. She had personal experience with that situation as she had grown up in the Rio Grande Valley and started school speaking only Spanish.

Hernandez knew that the Dallas School District had a complex history. The relationship between the elected members of the school board and the Superintendent of Schools was sometimes difficult. The board was composed of diverse individuals with Hispanic backgrounds, African Americans and Anglos. Until relatively recently, the superintendent was someone who had been in the system for many years. He had created a rigorous evaluation system that used performance and student results to measure principal effectiveness. There were also attempts to link student performance to assessments of teacher effectiveness. The school board members were not always supportive of these efforts.

She asked her faculty members at the LBJ School about the impact of the past policies in Dallas, especially the impact on students with bilingual language backgrounds.

Nobody at the LBJ School seemed to be able to answer her query. When she examined the contract that her employer had signed with the school district, it appeared that the consulting firm had emphasized their technical ability to use test scores for a range of issues. It was not clear to her whether there were different performance patterns for bilingual students and whether patterns such as dropout rates seemed to be related to test performance.

During her first few months in the role, Hernandez attended the meetings of the school board and observed that there was more attention to differential performance by African American students than to Hispanic students. She wasn't sure what that meant. She did observe that the superintendent was proposing that a number of schools be closed but she wasn't clear about the impact of that decision on Hispanic students.

Her consulting firm had been chosen by the school district because of its familiarity with the technical aspects of test scores and performance measures. But it didn't seem to her that those abilities really addressed the situation in Dallas. And she wasn't sure which party in the governance structure was her main client.

Lisa Li is a new Administrative Officer in the Hong Kong Education Bureau and has been tasked with an assignment from the Secretary for Education that involves the development of a five-year strategic plan for the Bureau. She realizes that this assignment is much more complex than she thought. She had developed a strategic plan for another part of the Hong Kong government but this position is her first involving the Hong Kong school system. She approached her assignment believing that most agencies develop strategic plans based on the projection of population patterns but are able to rely on past patterns as the basis for the new data.

In the case of Hong Kong, however, the projections are difficult to make because of two sets of uncertainty. One type of uncertainty emerges from the changing political relationship between Hong Kong and the mainland. It is possible that the Central Government may require Hong Kong (and Macao) to move its educational system closer to that found on the mainland. That could include requirements that deal with sensitive ideological differences between the two systems. They are expressed in the language of instruction, the curriculum and the relationship between Hong Kong and nearby provinces. In addition, the balance between public schools and private schools appears to be changing since increasingly mainland Chinese students are enrolling in the city's very expensive private international schools. Tuition fees for these schools are very high and mainland students have replaced the foreign students who traditionally attended the institutions.

The second type of uncertainty is related to the first but takes the form of population changes within Hong Kong. There is an increase in the number of foreigners who have come to Hong Kong to work in China's markets and take advantage of business opportunities. Between 2006 and 2016 the number of white residents has increased by 60 percent, many of them are from English speaking countries but others are German, Italian and French speaking. The increase in cost of the international schools has priced out that possibility for many non-Chinese families and the number of Caucasian students attending the city's public schools has increased dramatically while still being a significant minority. The majority of immigrant students enrolled in the public schools are Asian.

Currently primary public school students are required to use English and Cantonese in their regular classes but also learn Mandarin. High schools are usually designated either as English language or Cantonese language schools with other languages and Mandarin taught as electives. The British arrival in Hong Kong brought English into the school system but education was considered a service designed for the elite and the rich. The first government school that provided bilingual education in English and Chinese (Cantonese) was founded in 1890 but educating the poor did not become a priority until the poor were a majority of the population.

Lisa Li is trying to anticipate the views of the Secretary for Education and believes that it is important to achieve some agreement with that individual about the assignment. Since she hasn't worked with that person before, she doesn't know his preferences or assumptions about the assignment. She thinks that it will be important for her to discuss this with him. Before she meets with him, however, she expects to write a memo that lays out the following questions:

1   Does the five-year time frame make sense?
2   What assumptions should she make about the two areas of uncertainty?
3   Should she assume that the student composition will affect the educational approach used?
4   What kind of data is available for her assignment?
5   Should she be able to share her drafts of the memo and the final project with others in the system (especially the Social Welfare Bureau Director)?
6   Is this assignment known by others (e.g., the press, politicians, the educational sector)?

Veronica Lopez is a physician who has now become a policy analyst. She started her career working for the US Centers for Disease Prevention and Control (CDC) but soon moved to the Pan American Health Association (PAHO). Her focus on Latin America brought her to the Gates Foundation. In that position she became increasingly aware of the power of global health networks. She was recruited to join the staff of the World Health Association (WHO) less than a year ago.

WHO is a specialized agency of the United Nations that is concerned with international public health. Created in 1948, the organization is made up of nearly 200 member countries as well as organizations that have an observer role. It has been involved in a range of health issues across the globe.

During her tenure at the Gates Foundation, Lopez became aware of tension between the efforts of international health organizations (who operate through formal national structures) and the global health networks (whose activities involve a range of non-state organizations and approaches). She was brought to the WHO because of her knowledge about both types of efforts and the conflict that seemed to be increasing between them.

She felt that the two efforts were leading to a gulf between those who had expertise in major health problems and those who had formal authority to deal with those issues.

Her task at the WHO was to clarify the role that each of the groups played and to determine how they defined their audiences. She thought that the WHO's structure and formalism made them particularly sensitive to the political pressures that emerged from different countries. This was true despite the fact that the WHO regularly relies on experts not affiliated with states for consultation and formal recommendations. Those attributes also limited the consideration of alternative roles that might not constrain the WHO. She thought it would be useful for the WHO to think about the way it plays four different roles: (1) to establish norms for its members; (2) to enforce those norms as a regulator; (3) to play a research and development role (supporting research and pilot projects; and (4) to provide a forum that would involve both organizations and create a setting for them to share proposals.

Her initial conversations within the WHO suggested that some players were considering ways to turn the subject area/disease networks into larger structures that might be integrated into the formal organization. Some of those networks might replace existing structures.

But she also knew that many of the players in the networks felt that they were researchers who were at the cutting edge of many health issues, particularly those that occurred in low-income countries. They did not want to lose that ability.

Lopez realized that both of the groups probably contained actors with diverse perspectives. Thus she couldn't assume that either of them would be able to agree on a single alternative. Her assignment, therefore, required her to find ways to build coalitions both within and between them. In addition, the top leadership in the WHO would likely be skeptical about accepting what they might believe was a radical change in their activity.

She believed that her assignment did not only involve substantive changes in structure but also required her to be sensitive to the process that she would recommend adopting to make the changes.

James Marlin had been working on policy issues that affected rural residents for many years. Although he was working inside the US Department of Agriculture (USDA), over the years he realized that there were significant differences between the way that USDA defined "rural" and the way that other agencies and departments thought about rural issues. Fewer and fewer rural citizens were directly affected by the policies of USDA as corporate farming became more widespread. Instead, issues that involved education, infrastructure, economic development, health and environment had an impact on those citizens.

When a Republican president tried to find a way to provide some visibility and a few resources to Republican governors through the creation of state rural development councils, James thought he had discovered a new outlet for his concerns. He realized that there were other mid-level career public servants across the federal government who shared his perspective. The original concept of the initiative envisioned a relationship between the state councils and their federal counterparts in Washington. It provided enough discretion to the state councils to allow them to craft agendas that reflected their unique experiences in each state.

As a result, a group titled the Monday Management Group was formed. Career federal staff (mostly at the GS 15 level) came to the Monday sessions from Agriculture, HHS, EPA, Interior, HUD, Transportation and other agencies. Groups that were interested in rural issues from outside of the government also participated. A network of individuals concerned about the future of rural America was formed without the traditional federal formalism. Meetings were scheduled that included both the state councils (who had representatives from the federal government, state government, local government, private sector, non-profits and tribal governments) as well as the Monday Management Group participants.

Marlin realized that effectively the combined Washington-based and state-based participants had become a loosely defined network. While it had few of the attributes of traditional clients (defined by formal elements) that network served as his non-traditional client. It lacked formal accountability elements. It had no real budget, authority or formal structure. But it became his client.

As long as the participants in the Monday Management Group continued to attend the meetings, Marlin knew that the network would continue to exist. But when an administration changed and participants were drawn to other assignments, it was obvious that this network would evaporate. It was a challenge to Marlin to figure out a way to create an alternative client to keep the activity alive.

James Mason is a native North Carolinian who worked on the campaign staff of the successful Democratic candidate for Governor in the state in 2016. Soon after the election was over a panel of federal judges struck down North Carolina's congressional map, condemning it as unconstitutional because Republicans had drawn the map seeking a political advantage. The ruling was the first time that a federal court had blocked a congressional map because of a partisan gerrymander, and it instantly endangered Republican seats in the coming elections. Race issues were extremely important in that decision since the boundary lines of the map minimized the impact of African American voters.

Mason had been active in the state NAACP organization and was attempting to determine the next step in his career. He did have a job offer in the Governor's Office but wasn't sure that position would be an effective place for him to work on this issue. Historically, the North Carolina Governor's Office had one of the weakest roles of governors in the US. Until relatively recently, the Governor did not even have authority to submit a budget to the legislature and had limited appointment authority.

But Mason did not know what other positions might be available to him to work on this issue. He was not a lawyer nor an expert on voting patterns. He had worked with the North Carolina Legislative Black Caucus during the 2016 campaign but that organization did not have a powerful position within the legislature. The map that the panel of judges had blocked had emerged directly from the Republicans in the legislature.

Judge James A. Wynn Jr., in a biting 191-page opinion, said that Republicans in North Carolina's Legislature had been "motivated by invidious partisan intent" as they carried out their obligation in 2016 to divide the state into 13 congressional districts, ten of which are held by Republicans. The result, Judge Wynn wrote, violated the 14th Amendment's guarantee of equal protection.

The ruling and its chief demand that the Republican-dominated Legislature create a new landscape of congressional districts infused new turmoil into the political chaos that has in recent years enveloped North Carolina. President Trump carried North Carolina in 2016, but the state elected a Democrat as its Governor on the same day and in 2008 supported President Barack Obama. On January 18, 2018, the United States Supreme Court stayed the federal court order pending review by the court.

Mason is attempting to find a way to become involved in this process. However, he does need to find a position that allows him to work on this issue and deal with his personal values.

Patrick Nonet recently moved from a job with the provincial government of Quebec to the Canadian national government. He was widely known as an advocate for the bilingual approach developed in the Official Languages Act of 1969 in which French was declared an official language alongside English. He was a player in the unsuccessful Quebec succession movement and election in 1995.

The 1969 Act required that all government activities, court proceedings, and legislations be carried out in English, French or both. French is the official language in Quebec with most of the debates, legislation and court proceedings conducted in French. However, the law also provides for the use of English in Quebec. Even in provinces and territories where English is the dominant language, French is normally used for the benefit of the public and in line with the Canadian laws.

Over the nearly 50 years since the language policy was put in place there has been a decline in the proportion of Canadians who are using French as their native language.

Quebec has the highest number of French speakers in Canada both by the proportion of the population in the province and the proportion of the entire population in the country. A total of 79.95 percent of the population of Quebec speaks French as their first language while 95 percent of the Quebec residents can speak French. In all the other provinces of Canada, the proportion of the people whose mother tongue is not French but have knowledge of French range from between 28 percent and 0.22 percent. A total of 28.36 percent of the population of New Brunswick speaks French as their mother tongue, the second highest in the country. Nunavut, Alberta, Saskatchewan, British Columbus and Newfoundland have the smallest populations of French speakers with less than 1 percent of their population speaking French. On average 20.61 percent of the Canadian population speak French at home on a regular basis.

Nonet is reaching retirement age and was brought to Ottawa to head up the staff of a Prime Minister's commission that will examine the future of the existing language policy. Given the era of tight budgets the creation of the commission reflected the Canadian Parliament's belief that it is important to determine whether this policy should be continued in its current form. Nonet is responsible to a commission that is composed of representatives from all of the provinces as well as members of the major political parties in the Parliament. In addition, the commission will have representatives of the three prominent groups of aboriginal people formally recognized by the government. The chair of the commission is someone who is a close colleague of the current prime minister.

Nonet understands the economic rationale for a change of policy but is also sensitive to the symbolism of the requirements. He has not had an opportunity to sit down with the chair of the commission to work out a strategy for the process.

William O'Neill is a consultant in Canberra, Australia who has been contacted by several individuals who are a part of a loose array of groups and individuals who are all concerned about the removal of several elected members from Parliament because they had dual citizenship in both Australia and another country.

The concern about dual citizenship was long standing. It had spawned a House of Representatives form that required all elected members to prepare a Citizenship Register statement that provided that if any of these individuals had citizenship in another country, the member was expected to renounce that citizenship.

As he discussed the situation with the group that had contacted him originally, O'Neill realized that it was very difficult to determine the causes of this practice and removal action. For some members of the coalition, the issue was best understood as a partisan political problem since the removal of some of the parliamentarians destroyed the Liberal coalition that was in power and required the Liberal Party to find other parties for a new coalition that would allow them to maintain their power base. Others who met with O'Neill posed the problem as a legal issue, pointing to Section 44 of the Australian constitution that disqualified individuals with citizenship other than Australian from serving in the Parliament. Still others defined the problem as closely linked to both the past and current Australian policies on immigration and race.

O'Neill recognized that the problem and the legal requirements were clearly left over from Australia's colonial past. Although it achieved independence at the turn of the twentieth century, many policies and approaches were inherited from the British past since Australian citizenship is modeled on that of the UK. Until 1949, Australians could only hold the status of British citizens and the term "White Australia policy" was used to effectively bar people of non-European descent from immigrating to Australia. At one point, the Australian states had the authority to determine citizenship requirements. Since that time, Australia's citizenship legislation has been amended over 30 times, often responding to shifts in migration programs. The estimates of population increase resulting from immigration turned out to be much lower than actually occurred. The concept of multiculturalism became the norm replacing restrictions based on racial and ethnic differences. It was not clear how those restrictions had affected aboriginal populations.

By the early 2000s, the citizenship legislation increased residence requirements from two to four years and saw an introduction of a citizenship test. Migrants were defined as permanent residents and had access to the range of welfare, health and educational services available to other citizens. The advantages of citizenship involve eligibility for a passport and permanent government employment. In addition, the requirements of Australian citizenship include requirements to vote since Australia has mandatory voting. In recent years, however, Australia seemed to be following a trend set by immigrant-receiving countries of Western Europe. Critics have argued that the country is turning the clock back to less inclusive, welcoming notions of citizenship and multiculturalism.

O'Neill believes that the current removal of parliamentarians with dual citizenship actually touches on all three of these policy frames. However, he thinks that the combined complexity of all of these issues would be difficult to handle by one network or group. Yet the people he met with liked the idea of an umbrella approach to this problem, reflecting diverse values and approaches. He sees his assignment as including the following issues:

1 Should the group focus on a permanent structure of an organization (officers, staff, membership requirements)?
2 How will it make decisions?
3 How will it establish priorities? Should it begin with low-hanging fruit?
4 How will it define its strategies?

George Smith was the first person in his family to complete a masters degree at a university. He had attended the University of West Virginia and took advantage of a program in public policy available on that campus. That educational achievement meant that he was the first male member of the family who was not working in a coal mine by the time he reached voting age. He had grown up hearing stories about his grandfather's leadership position in the Mine Workers Union. His grandfather was one of the top officials in the union who had been involved in the creation of the health system established to provide medical services for families that had a family member working in the mines.

While Smith knew that globalization and alternate energy products meant that it was not likely that coal mining would ever return to its position in the state economy, he found it difficult to listen to those who argued that coal mining was dead. He was concerned that the critics of the industry did not acknowledge the contributions that the workers and owners of the mines had made to the state and its citizens. He felt that those critics had written-off the work, life and sometimes death of five generations of his family.

During the 2016 presidential election it was difficult for him to see how he could use his personal involvement with the coal industry in the political debate. He was reluctant to speak about his personal and family views on coal mining but was skeptical about supporting the promises that Trump had made about reinvigorating the coal industry. He felt that these promises were not realistic and actually were an attempt to manipulate votes.

At the same time, Smith did not think that many Democrats were able to think realistically about the future development in the state. Population shifts indicated that younger people were leaving the state, often because educational opportunities were not available to them. At the same time, he found it difficult to support Democrats who had not tried to anticipate these problems.

But he was attracted by the efforts of teachers unions within the state to increase funding for teachers and educational programs. While the budget situation was not very optimistic, he thought that attempts to increase funding would provide the beginning of an agenda for the future. But it wasn't clear to him how he could use his training to work on this agenda. Who was likely to hire him?

Margaret Trumball recently moved from the UN headquarters in New York to the European Commission headquarters in Brussels. Soon after she made the transition she was assigned to the migration policy unit in the commission. The client for her analysis – the head of the unit – was relatively new to that position; he was from one of the countries that was a newer member of the European Union. They were largely drawn from former Soviet Union countries. The migration policy unit replaced someone from France (one of the original members of the EU) with someone from Poland.

Although both the UN and the European Commission are organizations composed of multiple perspectives drawn from different countries, Trumball realized that the two organizations seemed to operate in very different ways. She knew that the old timers at the commission identified themselves as international civil servants who responded to the hierarchical structure of the organization while the newer staff brought experiences and approaches that had been developed during the Soviet era. In addition, she knew that migration policy issues were especially problematic for countries such as France, Italy, Greece and other countries that had close borders with Africa and the Middle East.

Trumball was puzzled by this situation. Could she find a way to distribute responsibility among the EU members in a way that acknowledged their differential concern about the migration issues? What analytic techniques seemed to be helpful in finding a way to distribute responsibility among members and yet devise a clear policy? The issue itself raised strong views that transcended boundary lines.

She thought that the situation suggested that her product as a policy analyst would not make a single recommendation to the client but, rather, would provide alternatives to be considered by the client. She also thought that she might consider conceptualizing her client as a part of a loose network of groups and individuals concerned about migration issues. In fact, she thought that she might attempt to broaden the players, looking beyond the EU membership. She thought that it was important to discuss these possibilities with her commission client at the beginning of the process.

WANG Liping is on the staff of the President of the Peoples' Republic of China. Over the past few years he has been assigned to work on environmental issues and has accompanied the President to the United Nations Framework Convention on Climate Change in Paris (the Paris Agreement) in 2015. While he began his involvement with the environmental issue as an international problem it became increasingly clear that it had significant domestic impacts that varied in terms of impacts on different provinces and industries. This variation involves both political and economic perspectives.

In addition, WANG has been asked to develop a policy position on this issue that reflects the three roles of the President – the administrative role as President, leader of the Communist Party and commander in chief of the military. He knows that each of the roles focuses on different aspects of an already complex issue.

He has put together an informal advisory group that will provide him with the views of a range of actors. Each of these actors has its own formal or informal think tank that should be able to articulate the concerns of their perspective. He has asked each member of the advisory group to prepare a position paper that outlines its own concerns as well as areas in which they might have either disagreement or agreement with other players. WANG knows that his choice of actors may be criticized but feels that this is one of the few ways for him to map the dimensions of the issue.

Members of the informal advisory group include:

1   *Development Research Center of the State Council.* It is a state agency responsible for policy research, strategic review and consulting of issues related to the economic and social development on mainland China. It is an advisory body which recommends policies to CPC (Communist Party of China) Central Committee and the state council.

2   *Ministry of Ecology and the Environment think tank.* The ministry prioritizes environmental protection issues in somewhat unusual ways. It has published rankings such as "worst 10 cities."

3   *Hebei Provincial Government think tank.* The Hebei province is in north central China and is a highly-polluted, old-industry province.

4   *Yunnan Provincial Government think tank.* A province that has significant economic reliance on tourism from nature reserves. It also has activity based on several international environmental NGOs.

5   *The Chinese Academy of Governance-Party School of the Central Committee.* A think tank that focuses on the education and training of top-rank party cadres and provincial senior officials.

6   *Chinese Academy of Social Sciences.* Considered to be the premier and most comprehensive academic research organization in China.

WANG has asked each of these actors to include the following in their submission to him:

1   Their definition of the policy problem, its origins and major players
2   Relevant past experience
3   Possible options
4   Constraints involved in adopting and implementing proposals

For several years **Jonathan Weston** has served as the chairman of a government affairs committee of the Association of Windmill Manufacturers. His role meant that he was closely monitoring the legislation that was developing in the US Congress as well as how the US Department of Energy was implementing legislation that had already passed. His familiarity with this policy area was well known. Thus it was not surprising that following the 2016 presidential election his name was on a short list to be a political appointee within the Department of Energy dealing with alternative energy approaches.

The approval process was very smooth. The job did not require Senate confirmation but it did assume that the candidate's background would be vetted by the White House and others. Members of the Senate and their staffs were likely to be consulted about the candidate. Thus within a month of the inauguration, Weston assumed his new office.

Many of the issues that came before him were very familiar. He knew that US windmill manufacturers were concerned about competition from companies in other countries. He had testified before Congress many times opposing what his organization viewed as a regulatory burden on the private sector. He believed that the industry needed flexibility to be a viable manufacturer.

But while these issues were familiar, he began to realize that his new role required him to look at them in a new way. The memos that were written by the career staff members raised issues that were quite new to him. The alternatives that were developed in these memos included the perspective of players that he had never considered in his earlier activity on the issue. Analyses by the career staff discussed trade-offs between a number of issues that came to light during the protracted budget process and involved a range of other players both within the Energy Department, other federal agencies (such as EPA and the State Department), and a range of other interest groups.

In the past Weston was comfortable complaining about what he called "administrative burdens" imposed by the federal government on the private sector. After several months in his new job, serving as the client for career staff analysts, he realized that the regulatory measures that he had opposed may actually be appropriate for the public sector role. He was shocked when several members of the career staff praised him for "going native."

James Williams was assigned to a new policy analysis unit in the Prime Minister's Office in Great Britain. The unit had been created as a result of a recent Parliamentary election. The Labour Party was able to devise a coalition government that had a narrow majority but was likely to face another election in the near future. The leadership in Labour was not secure and was worried about its ability to maintain power given that its coalition partners were not always in agreement with Labour.

Williams had been assigned to the unit developing the budget. His specific assignment was to come up with a research budget for colleges and universities that could be defended in Parliament and was based on a rational analysis. Williams was warned that an earlier Labour government had tried to base its budget request for educational research on criteria that emphasized research production rather than teaching. Each institution prepared standard statistical and narrative material for submission to central panels for assessment. A five-point criterion referenced scale was established that considered all types of research (applied, strategic and basic). The process was designed to reward and promote high quality efforts.

That earlier experience had not generated the results that its designers expected. It appeared that a conflict between perfectionists (who focused on the best research) and the pragmatists (who linked research to teaching and undergraduate classes) emerged. The Association of University Teachers criticized the process for contributing to the closure of departments and fields that emphasized the goals of the pragmatists.

In addition, the past process produced what many viewed as problematic; it was a distribution that did not spread resources across the range of both elite and non-elite institutions. This led to "creaming" to a few elite institutions and generated criticism from Labour Party voters who were concerned that the allocation process led to over-measured research and inadequate measurement of teaching. It was clear that the bulk of the funds went to the elite institutions and were not allocated to the less elite institutions.

Williams was concerned about repeating these problems if he tried to turn a highly formalized measurement process into a mechanized decision process. But he was concerned that he did need to employ a strategy that seemed rational to all players. He was not sure how to deal with the assignment and he didn't know how his client would approach the problem.

Marianne Williams just completed her third year working for the Baltimore Police Department on their Performance-Stat effort. She started working there during the internship that was a part of her MPP at the University of Maryland. The effort was started by the Mayor of Baltimore as a way to ensure that the Baltimore Police Department was performing according to the expectations of the Mayor and the city council.

By the second year of her experience she began to see differences in performance by police staff located in different parts of the city. She also was exposed to a literature about street level bureaucracy. That was a literature that emphasized the independence and variation that occurs in public organizations when staff are not located in a central place and, as a result, these individuals vary in the extent to which they enforce the rules and laws assigned to them. She was working for the police department when racial issues generated a difficult atmosphere in parts of the city with low-income residents. The death of Freddie Gray – an African American who died in police custody – became a focusing event in the city.

Williams saw that the Mayor and city council tended to emphasize data that described city-wide patterns of behavior rather than data that indicated differences across the city that might have resulted from diverse populations and very different settings. She was skeptical about the ability of the Performance-Stat process to find ways to control behavior and identify ways to address citizen needs. She didn't think that the current view of one-size-fits-all was the path to take. When her office became an information source for budget allocation decisions, she thought that this might be an alternative way to act on her analysis.

She was still early in her career and wasn't sure how to use the experience she had developed over the past few years in her next job. Was there someone in the city government who shared her views? Could she find a way to identify such an opportunity? Should she explore possibilities in the Mayor's Office or the city council? Were there groups of citizens and officials who were trying to address the issues that led to the death of Freddie Gray? Could Performance-Stat be helpful in meeting that agenda?

James Williamson has been recently hired by a consortium of foundations that supported higher education programs for students from families who did not have the resources to pay for college for their children. The consortium is 20 years old and is made up of seven different foundations that provide a variety of resources to approximately 12 state higher education agencies across the US. Williamson serves as the director of the consortium.

While new to this job, Williamson was quite familiar with its activities. Over the past 15 years, he had been employed by two of the state agencies that received funds from the consortium. He was a senior staff member in one of the states and director of the staff in another state. Although both states attempted to reach similar goals, Williamson was struck by the differences between them in terms of their past experiences, the pathways they took to achieve the same goals, and their relationship with the consortium. It was clear to him that the consortium had been flexible in terms of their expectations about the use of the funds and effectively allowed states to define their own path.

Williamson's past experiences in the two states in which he had worked made him sensitive to differences in the structure of the state government, the demographic composition of the population in the state and the financial conditions that set the context for allocation of expenditures. While political changes were found in both states, they led to different pathways that represented the unpredictability of the institutional setting. Plans that had been developed were modified because of issues that emerged mid-stream. He also noted that the two states focused on different stages of the policy process: one highlighted the implementation of existing programs while the other emphasized the development of new programs and policies.

Williamson's new job as director of the consortium required him to define expectations about the use of the consortium's funding. While there was some pressure within the organization (especially its board) to establish a single model of expectations, his personal experience suggested that a one-size-fits-all approach was not likely to be effective. In addition, it was clear to him that each of the individual foundations in the consortium had different expectations and a variety of past experiences. At the same time, Williamson wanted to be able to report on the performance of the states in the program but he was skeptical about using traditional performance reports. Outreach and process strategies were not usually included in performance analysis yet they seemed to be important techniques.

He thought that whatever he did should be achieved collaboratively with the involvement of the state grantees and be sensitive to the different players and circumstances that each of them faced. He considered beginning his activity by creating a list of all of the types of approaches that had emerged over the past 20 years. This list would illustrate the diverse (and legitimate) approaches that had been used and provide a framework for the future. Such a list could be a way for the state agencies to explain what they would do in the future and, at the same time, justify their proposal. Such a list could also indicate what would not be allowed.

Williamson thought he should create planning working groups that included the grantees, consortium staff and board members. He wasn't sure how to begin the process; should it be framed as a clear process or developed incrementally?

Ellen Winston completed her masters in public policy with a clear policy focus. She knew that she wanted to organize her career around welfare policy issues. She found a paid internship for the summer between her first and second years in the academic program in the office of one of the major advocacy groups on welfare issues. She managed to focus on welfare policy in assignments for classes and kept up to date by reading reports and proposals that emerged from various organizations in the field.

After graduating she had the choice of jobs with three different interest groups that she admired. She chose the organization that had a separate policy analysis unit that was committed to developing reports and research efforts on topical issues. That unit had recruited staff who were experts on welfare policy issues. She felt that this staff added credibility to advocacy work by grounding it in evidence. That work provided the basis for options for the leadership of the organization and also influenced positions for other organizations in the field.

After about six months in the role, Winston realized that the structure of the organization had an impact on the substance of the proposals that emerged from the policy unit. She noted that both the policy analysis office as well as the lobbying office reported to the same vice president. That individual attempted to blend a staff that used diverse approaches. The lobby staff saw the effort as helping the lobbyists develop alternatives that would generate support in Congress, in state and local settings, and in other organizations. In contrast, the policy analysis group saw the mission as furthering knowledge in the field. The two units also had very different clients.

While Winston understood the diverse goals of the two units, she was uncomfortable with the focus on political realities and a short time frame. She was not prepared for the differences between the lobbying and research effort and the competition between them as they sought resources from the larger organization.

She realized she needed to focus on one of the two approaches. Her research orientation often was constrained by limits of resources, time and support. She believed that she might want to consider a more academic setting even though it was unlikely to directly produce policy alternatives.

Joyce Winter is a well-known policy analyst dealing with environment issues in California. She has had a range of positions at both state and federal government levels and, as well, has worked with a number of environmental public interest groups. She is recognized as an important player in the development of California leadership in the environmental field.

By the second year of the Trump administration it became clear that conflict between California policies and federal government policies was becoming more intense. It seemed that federalism was being defined in new ways. The Constitution and past policies had given states the ability to avoid regulations and minimize government control; the current experience suggested that some states chose to develop policies, particularly in the environmental area, that emphasized regulation and government control. Given the population size and economic influence of California, the conflict threatened those in power in the federal government.

As she thought about these issues, Winter realized that it was time to develop a strategy before Governor Jerry Brown left office. She also knew that former senator Barbara Boxer was concerned about these issues and was still active in the state. The current California delegation in the US House and Senate was likely to be interested in some strategy that encouraged other states to join California on environmental issues.

Winter knew that the situation called for an atypical policy analysis approach – one that helped to put the issue on the agenda. But she wasn't sure whether it made sense to create a new organization, commission a study or a book on the issues, or identify prominent Californians who would be leaders in such an effort. She was especially concerned about the attack on science that seemed to be associated with the California values. She thought that it would be possible to raise funds for some effort but it wasn't clear whether she would be competing with other issues (e.g., immigration questions).

Should she try to write a call for action and use that as a way to identify Californians who would be a part of such a movement? Does she have a client for her strategy?

Bibliography

Bardach, G. and Patashnik, Eric M., 2016, *A Practical Guide for Policy Analysis: The Eightfold Path to More Effective Problem Solving*, Fifth Edition (Washington, DC: CQ Press).

Benveniste, G., 1977, *The Politics of Expertise*, Second Edition (San Francisco: Boyd and Fraser Publishing Co.).

Bondanella, P. and Musa, M., eds., 1979, *The Portable Machiavelli* (New York: Penguin Books).

Brewer, Garry D. and deLeon, Peter, 1984, *The Foundations of Policy Analysis* (Belmont, CA: Wadsworth).

Commission on Evidence-Based Policymaking, 2017, Report of the Commission on Evidence-Based Policymaking, 2017, *The Promise of Evidence-Based Policymaking*, September (Washington, DC).

Dobel, P. and Day, A., 2005, "A Note on Mapping: Understanding Who Can Influence Your Success," *Electronic Hallway*, Evans School of Public Affairs, University of Washington, Seattle.

Dror, Y., 1984, "Policy Analysis for Advising Rulers," eds. Rolfe Tomlinson and Istvan Kiss, *Rethinking the Process of Operational Research and Systems Analysis* (Oxford: Pergamon Press).

Dror, Y., 1971, *Ventures in Policy Sciences* (New York: Elsevier).

Feldman, M., 1989, *Order without Design: Information Production and Policy Making* (Stanford, CA: Stanford University Press).

Fukuyama, Francis, 2018, "What's Wrong with Public Policy Education", *The American Interest*, published August 1.

Gawande, Atul, 2011, *The Checklist Manifesto: How to Get Things Right* (New York: Picador Publishers).

Gerth, H. H. and Wright Mills, C., 1946, *From Max Weber: Essays in Sociology* (New York: Oxford University Press).

Geva-May, I. with Wildavsky, Aaron, 1997, *An Operational Approach to Policy Analysis: The Craft* (Boston: Kluwer Academic Publishers).

Goldhamer, H., 1978, *The Adviser*, (New York: Elsevier).

Hale, K., 2011, *How Information Matters: Networks and Public Policy Innovation* (Washington, DC: Georgetown University Press).

Hogwood, B. W. and Gunn, Lewis A., 1984, *Policy Analysis for the Real World* (Oxford: Oxford University Press).

House, P. H., 1982, *The Art of Public Policy Analysis* (Beverly Hills, Calif.: Sage Publications).

Kingdon, John, 1984, *Agenda, Alternatives, and Public Policies* (Boston: Little, Brown).

Lindblom, Charles, 1968, *The Policy-Making Process* (Englewood Cliffs, N.J.: Prentice-Hall, Inc).

Lindblom, C. E. and Cohen, D. K., 1989, *Useable Knowledge: Social Science and Social Problem Solving* (New Haven, CT: Yale University Press).

Majone, G., 1989, *Evidence, Argument, and Persuasion in the Policy Process* (New Haven, CT: Yale University Press).

Malbin, M. J., 1980, *Unelected Representatives: Congressional Staff and the Future of Representative Government* (New York: Basic Books).

McGuire, M. and Agranoff, R., 2011, "The Limitations of Public Management Networks," *Public Administration Review*, 89:2, 266.

Meltsner, A. J., 1976, *Policy Analysts in the Bureaucracy* (Berkeley: University of California Press).

Meltsner, A. J., 1972, "Political Feasibility and Policy Analysis," *Public Administration Review* (November/December), 859–67.

Nakamura, R. and Smallwood, F., 1980, *The Politics of Policy Implementation* (New York: St. Martin's Press).

Nelson, R. H., 1989, "The Office of Policy Analysis in the Department of the Interior," *Journal of Policy Analysis and Management*, 8:3, 395–410.

Pressman, J. L. and Wildavsky, Aaron B., 1973, *Implementation: How Great Expectations in Washington Are Dashed in Oakland* (Berkeley: University of California Press).

Radin, B. A., 2016, "Policy Analysis and Advising Decisionmakers: Don't Forget the Decisionmaker/Client," *Journal of Comparative Policy Analysis: Research and Practice*, 18:3, 290–301.

Radin, B. A., 2013, *Beyond Machiavelli: Policy Analysis Reaches Midlife*, Second Edition (Washington, DC: Georgetown University Press).

Radin, B. A., 2000, *Beyond Machiavelli: Policy Analysis Comes of Age* (Washington, DC: Georgetown University Press).

Radin, B. A., 1997, "Presidential Address: The Evolution of the Policy Analysis Field: From Conversation to Conversations," *Journal of Policy Analysis and Management*, 16:2 (1997), 204–18.

Radin, B. A., 1991, "Policy Analysis in the Office of the Assistant Secretary for Planning and Evaluation in HEW/HHS: Institutionalization and the Second Generation," ed. Carol H. Weiss, *Organizations for Policy Analysis: Helping Government Think* (Newbury Park, Calif.: Sage Publications), pp. 144–60.

Radin, B. A. and Hawley, Willis D., 1988, *The Politics of Federal Reorganization: Creating the US Department of Education* (London: Pergamon Press).

RAND, Home page, www.rand.org.

Rein, M. and White, S. H., 1977, "Policy Research: Belief and Doubt," *Policy Analysis*, 21:1 (winter 1977), 239–71.

Rhodes, R. A. W., 1992. "New Directions in the Study of Policy Networks," *European Journal of Political Research*, 21:2.

Rivlin, A. M., 2015, Keynote Speech to *Friends of Evidence*, November 13, 2015.

Rivlin, A. M., 1998, "Does Good Policy Analysis Matter?" Remarks at the Dedication of the Alice Mitchell Rivlin Conference Room, Office of the Assistant Secretary for Planning and Evaluation, Department of Health and Human Services, Washington, D.C., February 17, 1998.

Robinson, W. H., 1992, "The Congressional Research Service: Policy Consultant, Think Tank and Information Factory," ed. Carol H. Weiss, *Organizations for Policy Analysis: Helping Government Think* (Newbury Park: Sage Publications), 181–200.

Robinson, W. H., 1989, "Policy Analysis for Congress: Lengthening the Time Horizon," *Journal of Policy Analysis and Management*, 8:1, 3.

Stone, Deborah, 1997, *Policy Paradox: The Art of Political Decision Making* (New York: W. W. Norton & Co.), p. 68.

Thompson, P. R. and Yessian, M. R., 1992, "Policy Analysis in the Office of Inspector General, US Department of Health and Human Services," ed. Carol H. Weiss, *Organizations for Policy Analysis: Helping Government Think* (Newbury Park: Sage Publications, 1992), pp. 161–77.

Vining, A. R. and Weimer, D. L., 2010, "The Foundations of Public Administration: Policy Analysis," *Public Administration Review*, ASPA.

Weimer, D. J., 2012, "The Universal and the Particular in Policy Analysis and Training," *Journal of Comparative Policy Analysis*, 14:1, 4.

Weimer, D. L. and Vining, A. R., 1992, *Policy Analysis: Concepts and Practice*, Second Edition (Englewood Cliffs, NJ: Prentice Hall).

Weiss, C. H., 1989, "Congressional Committees as Users of Analysis," *Journal of Policy Analysis and Management*, 8:3, 411.

Weiss, C. H., 1983, "Ideology, Interests, and Information: The Basis of Policy Positions," eds. D. Callahan and B. Jennings, *Ethics, the Social Sciences, and Policy Analysis* (New York: Plenum Press).

West, W. F, 2011, *Program Budgeting and the Performance Movement: The Elusive Quest for Efficiency in Government* (Washington, DC: Georgetown University Press).

Wildavsky, A, 1979, *Speaking Truth to Power: The Art and Craft of Policy Analysis* (Boston: Little, Brown & Co.).

Wildavsky, A., 1969, "Rescuing Policy Analysis from PPBS," *Public Administration Review*, 29.

Wilensky, Harold, 1967, *Organizational Intelligence: Knowledge and Policy in Government and Industry* (New York, Basic Books).

Williams, W., 1998, *Honest Numbers and Democracy* (Washington, DC: Georgetown University Press).

Wilson, J. Q., 1989, *Bureaucracy* (New York, Basic Books, Inc.).

Index

64024843R00102

Made in the USA
Middletown, DE
28 August 2019